D0378862

NOT IN FRONT OF THE CORGIS

BRIAN HOEY

NOT IN FRONT OF THE CORGIS

SECRETS OF LIFE BEHIND THE ROYAL CURTAINS

The Robson Press

First published in Great Britain in 2011 by
The Robson Press
An imprint of Biteback Publishing Ltd
Westminster Tower
3 Albert Embankment
London SE1 7SP

ISBN 978-1-84954-176-3

10 9 8 7 6 5 4 3 2 1
A CIP catalogue record for this book is available from the British Library.

Cover design by Namkwan Cho
Set in Garamond Pro by Namkwan Cho

Printed and bound in Great Britain by
CPI Group (UK) Ltd, Croydon, CR0 4YY

For Diana
Who Loves all Dogs (even Corgis)

CONTENTS

ACKNOWLEDGEMENTS

Anyone who attempts to write about the Royal Family soon learns the art of utmost discretion. The family themselves rarely give interviews, and then only under the strictest control. Senior members of the Household are similarly constrained, so it is left to the junior and mainly domestic staff to enlighten authors on the secrets of life in royal service – and then only when they are satisfied that their identity will be concealed.

As I have been writing about royalty for more than forty years, there is no one left at Buckingham Palace who was working there when I started. Therefore, many of the anecdotes and stories I relate come from former members of the Household, now retired – or even gone to that greater palace in the sky. Nevertheless, I remain bound by my original promise not to reveal my sources, and this applies equally to those currently employed by The Queen and her family, even though most of the tales are completely harmless and were told to me out of a sense of affection and amusement, rather than with any malicious intent.

The present Household is usually prepared to assist in correcting factual matters, but understandably its members are not willing to offer opinions – or gossip.

I am very grateful to all who have helped me in preparing this book and once again emphasise that, unless from quoted sources, all opinions – and errors – are mine.

At The Robson Press, the publisher Jeremy Robson commissioned the book, for which I am truly appreciative, while the Senior Editor, Sam Carter, has done a magnificent job in amending the text and making sure, with his colleague Clara Pelly, that my mistakes have been corrected. Namkwan Cho designed the cover and text.

At my agents, Curtis Brown, Gordon Wise and his colleague John Parton have handled all the necessary paperwork with their usual efficiency and kindness, while my grandchildren have rescued me with patience and tact when the intricacies of computers defeated me.

My thanks to them all.

Brian Hoey
Talygarn 2011

PROLOGUE

I was once in Buckingham Palace when I passed two young footmen whispering together in a corridor. I jokingly asked them if they were conspiring, to which they replied, 'Please Sir, not in front of the Corgis.' The expression was new to me. What they meant was that when they saw the Corgis approaching, they knew The Queen would not be far behind.

Because the dogs hold such an important place in Her Majesty's affections, the staff are careful not to offend them in any way, and they dare not utter a remark in Royal hearing criticising the animals.

The Queen's Corgi dogs are the most pampered pooches in the world. They are allowed unrestricted access to any part of any Royal residence; nowhere is off-limits. They travel with Her Majesty when she moves from palace to castle and back again and no one is allowed to touch them apart from their Royal mistress. If a visitor attempts to pat them, The Queen will sharply remind them that they do not like to be handled by anyone except her.

She insists on feeding them herself and they obey only her, no one else. The royal chef prepares their food. The proud boast is that none of The Queen's Corgis has ever eaten anything from a can; everything is cooked to order and when the bowls are placed in front of the animals, they never start until Her Majesty gives the word.

Once they have eaten, they have to be exercised in the gardens, rain or shine. If The Queen is free she likes to walk them and the rule for gardeners at work is that they should remove their hats when she passes (The Queen not the dogs) and not speak unless she talks first. She usually will have a few words.

If the Corgis decide to 'water' the flowerbeds, the gardeners are forbidden from stopping them. The Palace footmen loathe the animals, as they are yappy and snappy. They also are not fully house-trained so a supply of soda water and blotting paper is kept at hand just in case of any 'little accidents'.

It should come as no surprise to learn that royalty considers their animals more important than their servants. It's a throwback to medieval times when dogs and horses occupied a unique position in many aristocratic homes.

And in several other ways, the present Royal Family likes to preserve old-fashioned values. They prefer to distance themselves from their retainers, allowing them to get on with their lives in their own ways, on

PROLOGUE

their side of the green baize door – just so long as
nothing interferes with the family's comfort.

Buckingham Palace, which has been unkindly
referred to as a monument to the past, is one of the
few remaining households where an almost feudal
upstairs/downstairs system is maintained, with as
much adherence to precedence and protocol below
stairs as among the Royal Family themselves.

The senior of The Queen's domestic servants, the
Palace Steward, is as much a sovereign on his side of
the green baize door as Her Majesty is on hers. His
word is law and he is waited on hand, foot and finger
by a retinue of junior staff, actually greater in number
than the personal servants who work directly for The
Queen. His morning tea is served in the finest bone
china cup and saucer and no one would dare disturb
him when he is taking his afternoon nap.

The present Palace Steward started as a junior
footman and it has taken more than twenty years to
work up to his current exalted position in the Royal
Household. Nobody argues with him except perhaps
the royal chef, who works entirely independently in
his own little kingdom.

The Royal Family has an old-fashioned attitude to
its servants: patriarchal, benevolent and at times severe
if things are not done promptly. If a servant does not
do his or her master's or mistress's bidding quickly
enough, or has not carried out instructions to the
letter, the Royal's wrath is rapidly felt.

The tiniest things irritate members of the Royal
Family: an article being moved, furniture being
changed or repositioned without permission, or a

3

servant not answering a call immediately. And their attitude to their visitors can be equally confusing at times.

The late James [later Lord] Callaghan, when he was Prime Minister, was a frequent guest of The Queen Mother at Clarence House, and on one occasion, when there were just the two of them present, she was eating from an enormous box of chocolates when he arrived. She asked him if he would like one. When he said yes, she then pointed to one in the middle of the box and said, 'Have that one,' which he thought a little unusual. During the time he was eating his one chocolate, she ate three more and then invited him to have another, once again selecting the one he should have. This went on for the remainder of the morning, with Her Majesty always pointing to the ones he could have. As Callaghan left he spoke to The Queen's Page and asked why he was offered only those particular chocolates. The Page let him in on the secret: 'Those are the ones with hard centres. Her Majesty only eats the chocolates with soft centres.'

When Prince Philip gives a private dinner, he likes to decide the subject for conversation. One lady was dismayed to find she was expected to contribute on the subject of 'deciduous trees', about which she knew absolutely nothing. If guests are not quite as knowledgeable as they should be, the Prince can become very touchy – but if someone is more expert than him, it can just as easily ruin the occasion. Apparently the secret is to contact his office beforehand and find out his pet topics of the moment and learn just enough to be able to contribute intelligently, but not to upstage the host. Otherwise he can become 'less than pleased'.

Another of his foibles emerges if, when watching one of his favourite television programmes, an expected guest arrives – and no others would be admitted. He will order his footman to give the man a drink and tell him His Royal Highness won't be long as he is involved in urgent business.

The Duke of York employs the same tactic when he has visitors he feels can be put off.

Prince Andrew loves television and his staff record any programme he fancies so he can watch it later. As he spends a great deal of time away from home, they reckon they have a backlog of some three years of programmes waiting to be seen, but he will not allow any of them to be deleted.

His chef is said to despair of his master's culinary tastes, with his preference for 'burgers and fries drowned in ketchup', but when guests are invited – usually his golfing cronies – they eat and drink the finest foods and wines; he is an excellent host. Andrew dresses better than his brothers, and his valets – he has two – say he prefers dark pin-stripe suits to any others. Some people have remarked on the fact that Andrew always appears to wear the same suit; it's simply because he orders several in identical patterns and materials. He likes them, so why not?

Prince Charles employs one hundred and thirty-three staff to look after him and Camilla, with more than sixty of them domestics: chefs, cooks, footmen, housemaids, gardeners, chauffeurs, cleaners and his three personal valets whose sole responsibility is the care of their Royal master's extensive wardrobe and choosing what he is to wear on any particular day.

A serving soldier (he is not called a batman but a soldier servant) based at Birdcage Walk, polishes the Prince's boots and shoes every day – he has fifty pairs each costing over £800 to make by Lobb of St James's – and a housemaid washes his underwear as soon as it is discarded. Nothing Charles or Camilla wears is ever allowed near a washing machine. Particular attention is paid to handkerchiefs, which are monogrammed and again all hand-washed, as it was found that when they were sent to a laundry, some would go missing – as souvenirs.

HRH's suits, of which he has sixty, cost over £3,000 each, with his shirts, all hand-made at £350 a time (and he has more than 200) while his collar stiffeners are solid gold or silver.

The Duchess of Cornwall will not attend a private function unless she has been sent, in advance, a copy of the guest list. And she has been said to demand that certain names are deleted. On one occasion, two were apparently struck off and those of her son and daughter added.

As we shall see in the following pages, the Royal Household is a self-contained community, described by The Queen herself (though how she would know is anyone's guess) as a tiny village in itself, with all the infighting, gossip, jealousies, back-biting and intrigue one might encounter in an Agatha Christie novel. Her Majesty was spot on in her description, wherever she got it from.

A number of suicides have occurred among the staff, usually because of a love affair that has gone wrong – either between a housemaid and a footman, or occasionally because two male staff have ended a relationship. Another problem experienced by certain long-serving servants (who have known no other life) is that they suddenly found they no longer had a job to do. They were not sacked but were quietly isolated in their rooms on the top floor, and couldn't face a future without the daily routine and protective blanket they were used to in the Royal Household. Old-timers at the Palace will tell you that working there is not just a job but a way of life. Once you get sucked in, it is very difficult to move away, even if you want to. In fact, for some of these men and women, it is a self-imposed life sentence, albeit in the most comfortable surroundings.

The present generation of younger staff are better educated than those who previously worked there, so the adjustment to outside life is not so difficult. They know how to operate a bank account, use an ATM, where the local supermarket is and how much a curry and chips costs. But there are still some older domestic staff at the Palace who have come to depend on it totally. They like the idea of a post office where there is never a long line waiting to be served, or a bank that opens twenty-four hours a day – and doesn't charge for foreign currency if you are going abroad. It is still nice to have your laundry and dry cleaning collected and delivered free of charge, and if you are senior enough, to dine in surroundings reminiscent of the best gentlemen's clubs.

One former Master of the Household, the man responsible for the domestic side of the Palace, said that he was relieved there was only one 'proper' Queen in Buckingham Palace, as, with the temperamental staff he had to cope with, he had over a hundred below stairs.

Nobody outside the Royal Household really knows the luxurious extent of the lifestyle of the Royal Family. Outwardly, they give the impression of being frugal and parsimonious – which they are, even though Princess Anne prefers to call it 'Good old-fashioned Hanoverian Housekeeping' – but it does not apply to what they eat, drink, wear, drive and ride. Every one of them, from The Queen down to Prince Harry, enjoys only the best that money can buy, even if they expect their staff to negotiate the most advantageous deals when ordering on their behalf.

As a family they take luxury for granted, and regard loyalty – in others – above all other virtues. Servants are expected to obey without question, and to stand and be verbally abused without answering back, even when they are clearly not at fault. And there are constant reminders that they are held in less regard than the furniture, which is priceless, whereas servants can be replaced at any time.

There is a little-known network of mega-rich friends, British and foreign, who fall over themselves to provide 'safe' houses for the Royals to hold private dinners and for them to attend weekend house parties in the knowledge that nobody outside the inner circle will be aware of who else is present and what goes on. The younger members of the Royal Family all have a select group of acquaintants who provide yachts and private jets for holidays, and the arrangements when they make these trips are amazingly detailed and complicated, in order to avoid press intrusion.

Even those who are not involved in royal duties, such as the Earl of Snowdon's children, are the beneficiaries of largesse which would be denied any ordinary man or woman. Sir Anthony Bamford, son of the man who founded the world-famous JCB earth digger company, owns an enormous estate in Gloucestershire and he has provided Viscount Linley, The Queen's grandson, with a 'cottage' (actually a pleasant four-bedroom house) in the grounds as a weekend retreat. A member of the Sainsbury family has done the same thing for his goddaughter, Lady Sarah Chatto, and her husband, on his country estate.

It's a well-documented fact that figuratively all traffic lights turn to green for royalty. When the Princess Royal travels by ordinary schedule train from her home in Gloucestershire to London (using her Forces Family discount card) it can involve up to seven different organisations, including police from three counties, railway, Royal Household, Royal Protection Department and road traffic organisations. The only concession made to her royal status is that the car meeting her is allowed onto the forecourt at Paddington Station, but this is for security reasons.

Of course, the Princess Royal is considered to be the most self-reliant of The Queen's children. She refused to allow her own children to be given titles; she was the first to be married – and then divorced, and, so far, the only one to become romantically entangled with one of her mother's servants.

As in other great houses, members of the Royal Family, past and present, have become involved with their staff on a personal basis. But only on one occasion in the past one hundred years at Buckingham Palace has this resulted in marriage. Tim Laurence, who began his Royal Navy career as a 'Season' officer on board the Royal Yacht *Britannia* – which meant he only worked during the summer months – progressed to become Equerry to The Queen for three years as one of her most trusted and personal aides, before hitting the jackpot and marrying the boss's daughter, Anne, the Princess Royal. Their wedding took place only a few months after she divorced her first husband, Mark Phillips, and then it was revealed that Anne and Tim had been enjoying a relationship for some time before it became public knowledge. Vice-Admiral (as he later became) Laurence has still not been entirely forgiven by some of the 'Old Guard' at the Palace who simply could not understand, or accept, how the daughter of the Sovereign could consider marrying such a junior member of the Royal Household – and not one from an aristocratic background either.

In June 2011, The Queen conferred the honour of knighthood on her son-in-law, making him Sir Timothy Laurence KCVO, a Knight Commander of the Royal Victorian Order, Her Majesty's personal Order of Chivalry, given only to those who have performed a special service to The Queen or her family. Many royal observers are still cynically wondering what 'special service' Tim did to warrant this honour.

So murder, mayhem, suicides, love affairs between men and women, men and men, women and women, above and below stairs. Jealousies and ambitions, jockeying for position as close to The Queen as possible – backstabbing, fawning and sycophancy – it's all here.

On the surface the pace of the Court of Elizabeth II is as unhurried and placid as that of her great-great-grandmother, Queen Victoria, over a hundred years ago.

But the difference between the staff of today and those of sixty years ago is unimaginable, with only the dress interchangeable. The idea that everyone is born to a particular role in life, which must never change, has disappeared, with social divides being bridged by many people from modest origins. These days the servants of The Queen at least have a grasp of realities that was missing in days gone by. The footman, who opens the door at the Privy Purse entrance, greets visitors with an easy courtesy, instead of the rigid formality of previous years. It certainly helps to break the ice for first time visitors who might be feeling a little apprehensive.

At the same time no one who enters Buckingham Palace is unaware of the magic of the place, the mystique of Monarchy that permeates the very air.

CHAPTER ONE

THE HOUSE

Buckingham Palace, or simply 'The House' as all the members of the Royal Family know it – Prince Charles pronounces it 'The Hice' – is the official London residence of the Sovereign. It is also the only home of the Royal Family that bears the name of its original owner: John Sheffield, Duke of Buckingham, who was 'persuaded' to sell it to King George III, the 'Mad' Monarch who is said to have 'given away' the American colonies. The price was considered, even in 1762, to be the property bargain of the century: £28,000, though it was not intended to be the principal residence of the Sovereign; that was to remain across the road at St James's Palace, still the Court to which all foreign emissaries are accredited.

Considering that Buckingham Palace has been in the possession of the Royal Family for just over 250 years, some of the legends that have taken root appear to have come from medieval times.

Every great house has a murder mystery and Buckingham Palace has one of its own, involving the then Shah of Persia. During a State Visit in 1873, a servant was supposed to be guarding the Shah's bedroom in the Belgian Suite throughout the night, but was discovered asleep on duty. His master ordered him to be beaten. The bodyguards took the order so literally that the servant died of his injuries. Queen Victoria was informed that it was a natural death and, to save unnecessary paperwork and any potential embarrassment, his body was (allegedly) buried secretly at dead of night, in a far corner of the Palace gardens near Hyde Park Corner, where, it is claimed, no flowers have blossomed since that day. Some of the more gullible young housemaids believe his spirit haunts the Palace and claim they have actually seen the ghost – at least that's the reason they give when found sneaking into a forbidden bedroom late at night.

On a more prosaic note, the guardsmen who march up and down in front of the Palace in their scarlet tunics and bearskins, with a rota of two hours on four hours off, night and day, could not do much to ward off any would-be attacks as their weapons are unloaded.

The only time when they have been issued with live ammunition was in 1936 when King Edward VIII announced his abdication. In those days the guard were stationed outside the gates and not where they are today and it was thought that certain elements of the crowds might try to storm the Palace. It never happened of course, but the soldiers are grateful that they now do not have to endure the taunts of visitors who want to be photographed alongside them and often used to try to make them laugh – which would have been against orders and would have meant the poor guardsman being placed on a charge.

The guards still occupy these exposed positions outside St James's Palace where the usual antics go on day after day. Apparently the Japanese are the worst offenders.

Buckingham Palace is quite simply the most famous address in the world. When President Obama arrived for a State Visit in May 2011 with his wife Michelle, he was astounded at the attention to detail that accompanied their two-day stay. The Palace officials had even found out what sort of toilet paper the Obamas preferred in their bathroom (thickness, consistency and colour), their favourite flowers and whether they liked sheets and blankets (wool or cotton) or duvets on their beds. As the couple left, they echoed the words spoken by a previous US President, George Bush Snr, when he said, 'Nobody does it better.'

Queen Victoria was the first monarch to live in the Palace when she moved in on 13 July 1837, just three weeks after her accession, and her successors have continued to occupy it.

But apart from George III, most of the monarchs who have lived there have not cared for the place. Indeed it was The Queen's grandfather, King George V, who first called it The House when he said, 'Sandringham [his Norfolk country estate] is my home; Buckingham

Palace is just a house.' From that date, all the Royals have referred to the Palace as 'The House'.

When King George VI acceded to the throne on the abdication of his brother King Edward VIII in 1936, he wanted to live at Clarence House, because he thought the Palace was no place to bring up two young daughters; Princess Elizabeth was ten years old at the time, while her sister Margaret was only six. It was Winston Churchill who insisted that the British people expected to see their King living in his Palace and virtually forced the new Sovereign to move, albeit reluctantly, across the road.

The Queen has never revealed her feelings about The House, but the impression that members of the Royal Household get is that she too regards the place as simply a necessary working location from which to carry out her role.

There is nothing very pretty or attractive about the Palace. It's a functional, Portland stone edifice containing the nineteen State Apartments open to the public since 1993, but only in the summer months when The Queen is not in residence. She refuses to have the hoi polloi around when she might bump into any of them. But if you know the right people it is not difficult to have a private tour, even when The Queen is at home. One or two of the staff are said to have 'arrangements' whereby visitors – only around three or four at a time, so as not to arouse suspicion – arrive at a prearranged hour and are discreetly shown around the State Apartments. And if, at the end of the tour, the visitors like to press a few notes into a waiting hand, it would be considered bad form to refuse.

When The Queen decided, against her mother's and Prince Charles's wishes, to open the Palace to the public in 1993, she first of all walked through every room choosing which apartments she would allow the people to see. Indeed, it took seven years before she would permit the State Ballroom to be included in the tour. And today some of the more interesting rooms are strictly off-limits to anyone but the Royal Family and their personal guests: the Chinese Dining Room, with its unique décor and the India Room next door, which contains a magnificent collection of weaponry, are just two that are forbidden territory because of their proximity to the Duke of Edinburgh's suite, while the Audience Room is far too close to Her Majesty's private sitting room – and also the special room reserved for the Corgis. There appears to be no reason on earth why the Belgian Suite on the ground floor, where important guests stay, could not be seen, but The Queen decided against it and no one argues with her.

Throughout the working week – that's Monday morning until Friday lunchtime – Buckingham Palace becomes the headquarters of Elizabeth II plc. It's just an unprepossessing office block, housing the various departments needed to service the administration of Her Majesty's official duties.

So, nineteen State Apartments, fifty-two bedrooms, ninety-two offices and ninety-eight bathrooms and lavatories (when Edward VIII lived here in 1936 there was only one bathroom and he scandalised the staff and his family by installing – horror of horrors – a shower), this is where affairs of State are handled and it is also the scene of the most lavish entertainment enjoyed anywhere in the world.

There are rules governing every aspect of life at Court, including entertaining. When singers, artists and musicians are summoned to entertain the Royal Family, they are given a seven-page document instructing them in how to behave. For example, they are told they must not, under any circumstances, slouch or lean against bars or tables, bow ties should be of the self-tie variety, as The Queen hates 'made-up' bow ties (she claims she can spot one at twenty paces) and performers are not allowed to speak to any member of the Royal Family unless spoken to first. If they are invited to a reception after the performance, they should never approach royalty without being asked – and escorted – by a member of the Household.

While most of the departments within the Palace have been modernised to a certain extent, with word processors replacing manual typewriters, and a computer on every desk – they are even used in the kitchens – there remains an air of quiet tranquillity throughout the building. I have only ever seen one person running in the corridors and that was The Queen, at 10 a.m., as she rushed from one room to another, dressed in formal robes and tiara. My companion at the time explained that she was on her way to a sitting with an artist and she never liked to keep anyone waiting. Punctuality is the politeness of princes – and obviously queens. Otherwise, the idea of anyone hurrying is unthinkable.

There is also a custom that office doors are kept open – and all the senior members: Private Secretaries,

Keeper of the Privy Purse, Comptroller of the Lord Chamberlain's Office, who are located on the ground floor, keep their doors open during working hours. No one knows why and how this began but it means a visitor will catch fascinating snippets of conversation as he passes by. And newcomers are warned to keep an eye open in case the Duke of Edinburgh emerges from his Private Secretary's office. Even at ninety, His Royal Highness rarely moves slowly and as he is often shouting back to someone over his shoulder without looking where he is going, there have been collisions. One visitor says that the first time it happened to him, the Duke bumped into him causing him to sit down suddenly on the carpet. They exchanged a few words, with Prince Philip's consisting of just two syllables, the second one being 'off'.

Buckingham Palace – and for the purposes of this book we will concentrate on the Palace even though there will be mentions of other royal residences – is a self-contained microcosm. No other house in Britain has its own bank, post office, police station, social clubs and separate apartments for different grades of staff. Also, with forty-five-acre grounds, it boasts the largest private garden in London.

The most senior members – and as we shall see in the chapter on the Royal Household, a Member, with a capital 'M', is not just another worker, but an important cog in the royal machine – are able to enjoy as much whisky, gin, brandy or any other drink as they like, free of charge, not that in these days of the breathalyser many of them are heavy drinkers, unlike in previous reigns when no meal was consumed without copious glasses of wine and champagne followed by liquers. A few years ago the Lord Chamberlain, on one of his rare budget-conscious saving sprees, decided to charge the Members for all the spirits they drank. It was then pointed out to him by the Keeper of the Privy Purse that it was costing so much to collect the money it wasn't worth the effort and the whole idea was quietly dropped – not that The Queen knew anything about it. If she had known she would have been highly amused. And there is no truth in the story that Her Majesty walks the Palace corridors at night switching off lights to save money.

Visitors to Buckingham Palace, apart from those who are invited to use the Grand Entrance, usually go in by the north centre gate, that's the one on the right as you face the Palace from The Mall. Once the policeman has checked your identity and verified that you are expected, you are directed across the gravel forecourt to the Privy Purse Door, so called because at one time it led straight into the office occupied by the Keeper of the Privy Purse. They have kept the name but that office is now used by The Queen's press secretary.

There are five shallow steps leading to the door, carpeted in rather shabby red carpet, worn thin by the hundreds of feet that use it continually. As you approach the door a liveried footman always opens it immediately; no one ever has to ring the doorbell or use the knocker. The footman wears his daytime uniform of dark green frock coat, black trousers, white shirt and striped waistcoat. They are the only men in the Palace who normally wear waistcoats (or vests), as

The Queen is believed not to care to see men wearing three-piece suits. If, as on the occasion of President Obama's visit, this is a State occasion, he will be wearing a scarlet tailcoat.

The footman greets the visitor by name and shows you into the waiting room on the immediate right of the front door. Furnished with gilt chairs upholstered in lime green silk, there are two writing tables but no writing paper or pens since guests began stealing them as royal souvenirs. Newspapers are laid out on a further small table and three large paintings, frequently changed, adorn the walls. There is a fireplace, but like every other fireplace in the Palace with the exception of the one in The Queen's sitting room, it is never lit. Altogether there are over 300 fireplaces in Buckingham Palace and as it normally takes some five people to prepare and light Her Majesty's fire, the practice has been quietly dropped and now central heating and single-bar electric fires have replaced coal and logs.

The system involving five people is as follows: the coal and kindling is collected from outside by a member of the garden staff, who hands it over to a kitchen porter (KP) as he is not expected to work inside the house. Then the KP carries the bundle to the green baize door separating the kitchen from the rest of the Palace and hands it on to a footman, who then carries it upstairs to Her Majesty's door. But he is not permitted to enter the private apartments so a housemaid then proceeds to take over and lays the fire, but, protocol being what it is, she does not strike the match to light the fire. That privilege goes to Her Majesty's personal Page. Obviously, if this were to be repeated throughout the Palace nothing would ever get done. So, modern central heating replaced coal fires and at the same time the environment was improved immeasurably, which, no doubt, would have greatly pleased Prince Charles.

When I first visited Buckingham Palace to discuss a biography I was proposing to write on Princess Anne (before she became the Princess Royal) I was allowed to walk around unaccompanied as long as I knew where I was going. These days, with health, safety and security precautions predominant, no outsider is permitted to move around without an escort. Not that anyone has ever been known to sue The Queen because they have fallen over or a painting has injured them, but the Palace is taking no chances.

If you are going up to see someone on the first floor, you will be taken in an antiquated lift complete with wood panelling and mirrors on the three walls. It creaks a little and moves at a snail's pace due to an order of The Queen who once instructed that it should be slowed down when Prince Charles and Princess Anne were very young – because, it is claimed, Anne liked to frighten her older brother as they rode up to the schoolroom, where the Princess Royal now has her private office. She also has the use of a comfortable apartment in York House, part of St James's Palace, when she stays overnight in London.

As The Queen never uses this particular lift, no one has thought to countermand her original instruction, made over fifty years ago.

Prince Andrew, Duke of York, has his office on the second floor of the Palace, where he receives official visitors, but his home is Royal Lodge in Windsor Great Park, which he inherited from his grandmother, Queen Elizabeth The Queen Mother, and which is distinguished by an aircraft ejector seat prominently displayed in the front hall. Visitors are invited to try it out but not to touch the ejector button! What The Queen Mother would make of her grandson's ideas on decoration is anybody's guess.

The top floor of Buckingham Palace is reserved for staff accommodation, with males at the right-hand corner, females on the left and newcomers at the rear. They move nearer the front the longer they work in the Palace. The rooms are spacious, furnished with heavy, dark wardrobes and dressing tables, and single beds only. Married couples do not occupy any of the rooms within the Palace; they have 'Grace and Favour' apartments elsewhere.

However, many of the staff have now been moved away from the Palace proper to accommodation in the Royal Mews because it is believed to be easier to secure.

One disadvantage to 'living in' is that there are no private *en suite* bathrooms for staff, so there is sometimes a queue in the early morning. It was during the heat wave of the summer of 1976 that the then Master of the Household was doing his rounds when he heard sounds of jollity coming from one of the staff bathrooms (there are no locks on the doors either.) On looking in he found two young footmen enjoying themselves together. When he demanded to know what they thought they were doing, one replied coolly that they were merely obeying his orders to save water. The Master was so impressed by this that both men kept their jobs – and he dined out on the story for weeks.

The domestic staff like to tell of some of the initiation rites newcomers were forced to endure when they first joined the Household. One involved running naked through the State Apartments late at night, hoping no one would see you. If you weren't caught, you were in. When The Queen's children were single and still living at home, they liked to witness this particular ceremony (unseen) and they never gave the culprits away.

The Queen's private apartments – bedroom, sitting room, dressing room, bathroom and dining room – are located on the first floor above the Garden Entrance overlooking Constitution Hill. They are easy to recognise, as they are the only ones on that side of the building with bow windows, and are usually the only ones late at night with lights still burning. Opposite is the Pages' Room, where her senior servants wait until called and next door to them is the Corgis' Room containing not only the beds for the dogs, raised slightly off the floor to avoid draughts, but also the spotlessly clean and polished bowls used to feed them.

Immediately above The Queen's suite, adjacent to Angela Kelly's (her senior dresser) apartment is Her Majesty's wardrobe, a large, cedar-lined room, containing not only the everyday outfits but also the magnificent formal robes worn at the State Opening of Parliament.

The Duke of Edinburgh's suite is adjacent to The Queen's, but separated by Her Majesty's bathroom.

When Michael Fagan broke into Buckingham Palace on 9 July 1982, and was discovered, dripping blood from a cut thumb, sitting on The Queen's bed when she woke up in the early morning, many of the tabloid press concentrated on the fact that she slept apart from Prince Philip. What they failed to realise is that with many couples of their generation and class it is perfectly normal for couples not to share a bed at all times.

One other reason in their case is that they have different preferences for bedclothes: The Queen likes a longer turn-back on her sheets and blankets, and lace trimming on her pillowcases; Prince Philip does not. And, as he was brought up in the rigid Puritanism of life at Gordonstoun, where cold showers and stoicism were the order of the day, he sleeps with his windows wide open whatever the weather and temperature. He has never used a hot-water bottle in his life. Added to which, even at ninety, His Royal Highness has his own agenda, so he frequently rises extra early and would not wish to disturb his wife. Above Prince Philip's bedroom is a fully equipped barber shop, where his hairdresser trims the royal locks once a week, and even provides a pedicure when needed.

Even when the royal couple had the use of the Royal Yacht *Britannia*, they had separate cabins and nowhere on the Yacht were there any double beds. When *Britannia* was used for royal honeymoons, the crew (known as Yachties) would rope two single beds together.

Two of the nicest apartments in the Palace are those that traditionally belonged to the Chief Housekeeper and the Superintendent of the Palace. These flank the principal entrance on the ground floor and are guarded by the soldiers on Palace sentry duty. However, neither of these apartments is now used as living accommodation. The Superintendent's position has been abolished, while the Chief Housekeeper now lives in a small apartment on the top floor overlooking The Mall. Their former quarters are now used as offices.

One of the many rules governing Buckingham Palace is that the lace curtains at the front are never drawn back, on the explicit instructions of The Queen who likes to preserve the 'Chocolate Box' effect of its appearance from the outside.

One young housemaid hung her underclothes out to dry from her window on one occasion. When the Master of the Household saw it he blew a fuse and ordered the offending garments to be removed from the windowsill immediately, even though the girl's room was at the rear of the Palace overlooking the inner quadrangle, so no one would have seen it from the front.

The nineteen State Apartments, used for formal occasions, including the wedding breakfast and reception following the marriage of Prince William and Catherine Middleton, are all situated on the first floor, reached via the Grand Staircase.

The first room is the Guard Chamber, a small anteroom where, in previous reigns, an officer would be stationed to check the credentials of anyone visiting the sovereign before allowing them to proceed.

From here, one is shown into the Green Drawing Room, where, as the name implies, the walls, ceiling and even the chairs are all in that colour. It is the central apartment on the west side of the Palace and in Queen Victoria's day, this was where the royal party would emerge to wave at the crowds in front of the Palace and along The Mall. Of course, Buckingham Palace was U-shaped then, without the north front wall that was erected after Marble Arch was removed, stone by stone, to enable Victoria to see – and more importantly – to be clearly seen by her people without any obstruction.

The Throne Room next door contains the throne chairs of The Queen, Prince Philip and those of previous reigns dotted around the room. On the evening of Prince William's wedding, his brother Harry took over the room and transformed it into a disco for the younger guests who had not been invited to the official wedding breakfast. Surely the only time such an event had been held in this august setting? One could almost feel the disapproving glare of Queen Victoria.

The Blue Drawing Room, which used to be called the South Drawing Room, is said by many visitors to be the most elegant of the State Apartments, but others claim it is too cold and impersonal. The blue flock wallpaper was installed by Queen Mary at the beginning of the twentieth century and the floor-to-ceiling Corinthian columns were painted to resemble onyx in order to cover up defects in the scagliola during the reign of Queen Victoria. The aim of King George IV and his designer Nash was to create an aura of extreme opulence and no one could deny that they succeeded. The Music Room contains the grand piano that has been played by Nöel Coward and Andrew Lloyd

Webber, among others, but since Princess Margaret and Diana, Princess of Wales are no longer with us, no other member of the Royal Family plays it. The Music Room has also been used for a number of royal christenings since enemy bombers in the Second World War destroyed the Chapel Royal. The White Drawing Room is the most welcoming and warm in the Palace, where the predominant colour is in fact not white but yellow. In one corner is a large fixture containing a full-size mirror and when a function is being held, a footman is stationed alongside. At a signal he presses a button and the entire fitment swings open to reveal the Royal Family who have been waiting in the Royal Closet, a small drawing room hidden behind the mirror, to have their own pre-function drinks: gin and Dubonnet for The Queen, whisky and soda or a sweet German wine for Prince Philip, Coke or orange juice for Princess Anne. The tableaux can surprise new guests who have not been let into the secret of the swinging mirror and more than one lady has found to her confusion that, instead of her own reflection, she sees the entire Royal Family looking back at her.

The Picture Gallery and Cross Picture Gallery are two more of the State Apartments brought into use when a reception is being held, and the State Ball Supper Room was the one used for the Wedding Breakfast of the Duke and Duchess of Cambridge. It is an elegant room and only the immediate families and the other royal guests were asked to sit here. The rest of the 600 invited back to the Palace used the other apartments, with the main State Apartment being the State Ballroom, built at a cost of £250,000 in 1848 by

Queen Victoria. Well, she didn't actually lay any bricks of course, but she did order its construction. It is the largest single private room in London and at today's prices would cost around £25 million.

Several State Apartments are never open to the public, including the Chinese Dining Room, the Buhl Guest Suite and the Balcony Room, from where the royal party emerge to wave to the crowds following a celebration such as a wedding or the State Opening of Parliament.

On the ground floor, the Belgian Suite is where foreign Heads of State are housed during visits to London and this leads onto the swimming pool.

Diagonally opposite on the ground floor is the Court Post Office across the corridor from the Palace's Pay Office. There is still a Billiards Room that is no longer used for its original purpose, so it is used mainly for small drinks parties when a senior member of the Household is leaving. The Bow Room, leading out onto the terrace, contains some magnificent examples of china and porcelain and it is also where an endearing custom used to be maintained. Whenever The Queen was departing for an overseas tour, members of the Royal Household would gather in the Bow Room to bid her farewell and assemble again on her return to welcome her home.

As The Queen now always leaves from the Garden Entrance near her private quarters, this little ceremony no longer takes place.

Up on the second floor, in the front, in what used to be the Palace schoolroom, is the Princess Royal's sitting room and office suite – her bedroom suite is now in York House at St James's Palace – and the Duke of York's offices are next door with the Lady-in-Waiting's suite occupying the entire corner.

There is also a mezzanine floor overlooking The Queen's Gallery and Buckingham Palace Road. This is where the staff Dining Room is located. The kitchens, which take up more than half of the east side of the ground floor, are immediately beneath the Dining Room.

This then is the London residence of The Queen and, far from being a museum piece, there is seldom a day in the year when Buckingham Palace is not humming with activity.

CHAPTER TWO

THE BEST OF FRIENDS

If ever there was a relationship between an august royal figure and her servant that was truly unique it was that between Queen Elizabeth, The Queen Mother and her Page of the Backstairs, William Tallon.

William, who was known to the outside world, and to other members of the Royal Household, as 'Backstairs Billy' – though never that to Her Majesty, openly admitted that he was in love with his boss and claimed that she had a great affection for him, which was true.

He once said The Queen Mother treated him as a favourite adopted son, while his colleagues suggested it was more like a naughty puppy. She allowed him certain privileges, but he was never permitted to overstep the mark, and in fairness to him, he knew his place.

With his mass of flamboyant hair and immaculate bearing, William was easily the most recognisable member of the Royal Household, before or since.

He thoroughly enjoyed basking in the reflected glory that came with his association with The Queen Mother and he dined out at some of London's finest restaurants, on the strength of that association.

Journalists and authors plied him with invitations, which he accepted with alacrity. One of his favourite bars was in Duke's Hotel in St James's, just across the road from Clarence House. William was a regular and he claimed they made the best martini in the world. A barman would wheel a trolley to William's table and mix the drink in front of him, making sure it was almost neat gin, which was the way he liked. His intake was prodigious. Like his royal mistress, he was said to have 'hollow legs' and many of his hosts found it impossible to keep up with him. And, when he walked back to Clarence House, he was as steady as when he had left.

William Tallon joined the Royal Household as a trainee footman in the early 1950s. He was a great success and promotion was fairly swift. When King George VI died in February 1952 and preparations began for the (by now) Queen Mother to move across the road from Buckingham Palace to Clarence House, William was part of the advance party. Her Majesty didn't actually move until nearly a year later, and it is believed in the Royal Household that she had to be practically carried, as she was reluctant to give up the Palace. For the first six months of Elizabeth II's reign, she and Prince Philip lived in the visitor's quarters in the Belgian Suite.

By the time The Queen Mother had been 'persuaded' to move, Clarence House had been transformed into the elegant home it was to remain for half a century. William liked to claim that it was a combination of Her Majesty's and his efforts that produced the sense of taste without ostentation that was exemplified in Clarence House. Perhaps, here again, there was a little exaggeration on his part.

Her Majesty's Household included a Private Secretary, Sir Martin Gilliat, a Comptroller of the Household, Capt. Sir Alastair Aird and a Treasurer, Sir Ralph Anstruther, whose job was to try and keep control of The Queen Mother's spending – and also to pay the people who worked for her.

There were a number of secretaries who went by the old-fashioned title of Lady Clerks and a press secretary, the delightful, if slightly unworldly, Major Sir John Griffin.

These were the mainstay of the Household, with, of course, legions of domestic servants from housekeeper to footmen, scullery maids to Pages. As mentioned, William Tallon rose to become Page of the Backstairs, while his life-long friend, Reg Willcox, was Page of the Presence, an equally prestigious position.

Both William and Reg were quite open about their sexuality, and The Queen Mother, like most of the Royal Family, was relaxed about their relationship or that of any other members of the Household.

There is one often-repeated story that on one occasion, Her Majesty was waiting for her usual gin and Dubonnet, when she heard sounds of a loud argument coming from the Pages Pantry. Finally losing her patience she shouted, 'When you two old queens have quite finished, this old Queen would like her cocktail.' True or false; it makes a good story and having known both men, it could well have been the former.

When Reg Willcox died, he left his entire estate, which consisted mainly of property he owned, to William, who was bereft at the loss of his old friend and sparring partner.

The Queen Mother did not replace Reg as Page of the Presence. She was content just to have William at her beck and call and he was happy to devote the rest of his career to her.

Like all the other members of the Royal Family, The Queen Mother hated the thought of having strange faces around her. Her staff remained long after the mandatory retirement age, and only death brought an end to service.

William became closer and closer to Her Majesty, without the relationship ever becoming in any way the slightest bit improper, in spite of snide comments from some quarters – and not all from tabloid newspapers – that theirs was more than a platonic friendship. But, he did tend to exaggerate her feelings more than a little. And he did have a fertile imagination. While there was no doubt that they were the best of friends from the time he entered her service, to the day she died in 2002, no one would believe that she returned what amounted to his near worship. She liked him, obviously. But they both kept the relationship on a mistress and servant basis, Her Majesty made sure of that. However, if the media, and anyone else for that matter, wanted to believe theirs was a love affair, even in a platonic state, William was the last person to try and disillusion them. On his part, he was never heard to address her as anything other than Your Majesty or Ma'am. His demeanour was exemplary at all times and there was one occasion when he was blamed for something that was not his fault and which hurt him badly.

On 4 August 2002, members of the Royal Family gathered at Clarence House to celebrate The Queen Mother's 100th birthday. As was usual, the family assembled at the gate to acknowledge the greetings of the crowd and to watch the band of the Irish Guards march past playing 'Happy Birthday'.

William, as usual, was in the party, and he was seen wheeling Princess Margaret who was confined to a wheelchair. Her appearance shocked the onlookers. Her face was badly puffed and her arm was in a sling. No one had ever seen her in such a state, particularly as two weeks earlier she had attended Prince Philip's eightieth birthday party at Windsor when she had looked all right.

William was heavily criticised by the media for pushing her to the fore and allowing the public to see her in such an appalling condition, the result of a fall in the shower when she badly scalded her legs and severely bruised her face. The only comment he made was, 'Do you think for one moment that I would have dared to push her in that way unless I had first been ordered to do so?'

Obviously both The Queen and The Queen Mother knew beforehand about Princess Margaret's condition and they took the decision to allow her to be seen, and she herself insisted on sharing her mother's big day. But had she realised just how ill she looked it is likely that she might have had second thoughts as she was a woman who had been proud of her looks and she would not wish to be remembered in that condition. Her own children, David Linley and Sarah Chatto, were also at Clarence House on that day and they raised no objections, so William was absolutely blameless.

He was fastidious about his personal appearance. When he was out of uniform he looked like a man who had been dressed by Savile Row, and perhaps he was. Suppliers fell over themselves to give him whatever he wanted. His shirts came from Turnball & Asser in Jermyn Street and he would not wear shirts with button-down collars or button sleeves. He had a large collection of cufflinks that he liked to display, including several pairs given to him by the Prince of Wales. And as a finishing touch, he also liked to wear a silk handkerchief flowing from his breast pocket. He used to point out to the valets of the Duke of Edinburgh that their master was committing a sartorial mortal sin by wearing a white handkerchief with the top folded straight across.

Someone once said that William exemplified that great British tradition of non-gentlemen who tried to pass themselves off as the real thing – and nearly, but not quite – succeeded.

Always immaculately turned out, whenever we met for a drink, he would arrive with a little bag of 'goodies' for my wife – who he had never met. It was typically generous of the man.

He also liked to boast that he never once sat down in The Queen Mother's presence and that she never once invited him to. He did share drinks with her on many occasions, especially at weekends when they were at Royal Lodge. She used to ask him to have the same drink as her, gin and Dubonnet with the proportions being, two thirds gin, one third Dubonnet and plenty of ice. But he didn't care too much for Dubonnet saying it was too sweet for his taste. So when he poured the drinks, his was usually nine-tenths gin and just a drop of Dubonnet, just to please her.

In the latter days of The Queen Mother's life, when she was still fairly active, they would be driven down to Royal Lodge on Friday afternoons after luncheon (they refused to call it lunch) and when the senior members of the Household had left for the evening, it would often be just the two of them in Her Majesty's sitting room. Of course, there were other staff in the house: security guards, footmen, a chef, in case The Queen Mother wanted a snack, and a dresser waiting to assist Her Majesty when she retired for the night. But the Ladies-in-Waiting, including her niece Mrs Margaret Rhodes, daughter of The Queen Mother's sister-in-law, would leave for their homes.

After a few stiff drinks, William would put on some records of The Queen Mother's favourite music and occasionally they would dance. Nothing too strenuous, just the odd foxtrot or waltz. And when the staff heard the strains of the music they knew they should not enter the room. It was simply two old friends enjoying the memories of times past. But, even in these surroundings, neither forgot for a moment who the other was – it was mistress and servant, and that was the way both preferred it. And he still wouldn't sit down in her presence.

When the Court adjourned to Balmoral, William often tried to hide away at night because he wasn't all that enthusiastic about Scottish highland dancing, which is de rigueur at Balmoral. The Queen Mother's niece told the story in a book she wrote, that on one occasion when Prince Charles was still single, he had to search the castle to find William, because 'Granny wants you for the Gay Gordons'. This was in the days when the word 'gay' was used only to describe joy rather than its current sexual definition, so there was no hidden double entendre intended.

During his service at Clarence House, William was given the use of Gate Lodge, a small but elegant single-storey property just outside the gates leading onto The Mall, surely one of the best addresses in London?

The house was a treasure trove as William was given hundreds of gifts by members of the Royal Family and also by suppliers to Queen Elizabeth. There were paintings, photographs, and prints, including sketches of the actor Keith Michel in his role as Henry VIII for a BBC TV drama along with his six wives. The Queen Mother had been given the prints, but she couldn't find the right place for them so she passed them on to William. She also presented him with items to make up a large dinner service, giving him a plate or soup bowl every Christmas. She died before he was able to complete the set.

In the latter stages of William's service with The Queen Mother, the Gate Lodge deteriorated into appalling condition. The walls were dripping with damp, the roof leaked, the plumbing needed attention and the doors didn't close properly. But the Comptroller of the Household refused to allocate the funds required for the repairs and The Queen Mother had no idea what the problem was. William never told her; he just put up with it.

However, within six weeks of her death, he was evicted from the property as the Prince of Wales was taking over Clarence House and William was informed that Gate Lodge was needed as a ticket office for the opening of the five State Apartments. He was moved out with indecent haste and indeed, the Lodge remained empty and in the same state of repair for some years after The Queen Mother's death.

William was devastated to lose his beloved home, but Prince Charles came to his rescue offering him a Grace and Favour apartment in Kennington, part of the Duchy of Cornwall's estate, near the Oval cricket ground.

The death of Queen Elizabeth truly was the end of an era. Her Page of the Backstairs had lost not only his home, but also the woman he had regarded as a surrogate mother for over half a century. For most of his adult life, William had never known any other existence. Clarence House during the week; Royal Lodge at weekends and Birkhall, Her Majesty's home in the Scottish Highlands, during the summer months. His routine coincided with hers; the only time he took off was when he knew she was with her daughters or grandchildren. Princess Margaret thought the world of him, though she would occasionally have a joke at his expense. He didn't take offence and both Margaret and The Queen included William in their family celebrations. He once showed me his collection of Royal Family Christmas cards, which numbered over 200. He also told of the day, when Princess Margaret was still living as a single woman at Clarence House and The Queen Mother entered the drawing room to find her daughter and William sitting side-by-side on a sofa. She was obviously surprised as Margaret was known for her imperious ways and the idea of sitting with a servant would normally have been anathema to her. But the Princess then made William stand and explained to her mother that there was a hole in the sofa that offended her. So she ordered him to sit and cover the hole until she was ready to leave the room. He found nothing unusual in such a command – or if he did, he was wise enough to keep his own counsel.

Once The Queen Mother had died, William found his former colleagues in the Royal Household were not as welcoming as he had hoped they would be and he became a lonely and disillusioned man. He still enjoyed tea at The Ritz if invited but the light had obviously gone out of his life.

During the final years of William's life, his connection with the Royal Family was mainly confined to a weekly Sunday lunch with Lord Snowdon, The Queen Mother's former son-in-law. Queen Elizabeth retained a great affection for Snowdon even after he and Princess Margaret divorced and he was a frequent visitor to Clarence House.

When he heard about William Tallon's loneliness following his dismissal from the Royal Household,

Tony Snowdon telephoned him and invited him to lunch at his home in Kensington. It became a regular date and William told me that Tony (Lord Snowdon insisted that William use his Christian name) had been a true friend in his hour of need: 'His loyalty never wavered for a moment.'

William's health had been in decline for some years and he died on 23 November 2007. He was seventy-two. Just over a week later his funeral was held in The Queen's Chapel, St James's Palace. It was a ceremony meticulously planned by the man himself with every detail laid out: hymns, prayers, eulogy, order of service and final music.

More than 2,000 mourners applied to attend, with only 200 being admitted to the tiny church.

Lord Snowdon and his daughter Lady Sarah Chatto were there, but no other member of the Royal Family attended. His Master of the Household represented the Prince of Wales. The rest of the congregation was made up of the great and the good from the worlds of show business, the arts and high society.

Sir Derek Jacobi read a verse specially written for the occasion 'in Praise of Billy', while the actresses Phyllida Law, June Brown (Dot Cotton from *Eastenders*) and Patricia Routledge (Mrs Bucket of TV fame) joined in the singing.

As a final tribute as his Union Jack bedecked coffin was carried from the chapel, the rousing *Radetsky March*, one of William's favourite pieces, was played. He chose it to be played at his funeral after hearing it played at the wedding of Princess Anne and Mark Phillips. He would have loved the occasion.

Eight months after his death, many of William's treasures, given to him by The Queen Mother and other members of the Royal Family, were sold at auction. There were 700 lots and buyers were attracted from all over the world, some arriving in person to bid, others by telephone.

An optimistic estimate of the total price was around £200,000. When the final tally was counted, it amounted to a staggering £444,364, more than twice the original estimate.

A handwritten note from The Queen Mother to William asking him to pack two bottles of Dubonnet and gin for a picnic fetched £16,000. It was expected to sell for £3,000.

Another letter, this time from Princess Diana to William went for £5,000, while a further seven Diana letters fetched £15,000.

The bidding was frantic and frenzied with 1,000 people on the telephones competing with the 400 men and women who had crowded into the saleroom in Essex. Among the beneficiaries of the sale were several charities that William had supported.

The £400,000 would have made a huge difference to his retirement if he had sold them in his lifetime, but he always refused to cash in, even refusing offers, said to be around £1 million, to write his memoirs.

William Tallon lived his life with panache and *joie de vivre*. He wasn't always as popular with his colleagues as he was with his boss, and the senior aides to The Queen Mother – the upstairs staff – didn't trust him at all. But they were cautious in their treatment as they realised he had the ear of Her Majesty, and in royal circles, that's all that counts. The sixty-odd domestic staff at Clarence House were terrified of him and he said that when dealing with people below you in the pecking order it was more important to be feared than liked. He once told me that the secret of his success was that it didn't matter who you were or where you came from; it was what people thought you were and where they thought you came from that mattered. He manufactured a persona for himself that was completely at odds with his humble working-class background and he said The Queen Mother encouraged him to assume the mannerisms and demeanour of someone from the 'upper crust' – his words. But he added that he always knew his place in the system and never succumbed to 'Red Carpet Fever' like so many others.

CHAPTER THREE

WHO LOVES YA?

here has always been an unofficial popularity 'league table' within the Royal Household regarding who the servants – and the police – prefer working for. It's been a running gag for generations of staff. The table changes from time to time but surprisingly, the people that, to the outside world, appear to be the most arrogant, difficult and uncompromising usually come out at the top of the table.

The relationship between the Royal Family and their servants is difficult to define in that you rarely get the sort of comfortable master/mistress/servant familiarity that exists in some aristocratic families.

The Royals are reluctant to allow anyone outside the immediate family to get too close, with few exceptions. The Queen's former Nanny, the late Bobo McDonald, enjoyed a special relationship with Her

Majesty until the day she died and Prince Charles is on friendly terms with his closest servants, his valets. But they know they should not confuse friendliness with familiarity. Royalty's apparent friendship with their servants is, inevitably, temporary, usually lasting only for the duration of the employment, and there is also a slight air of patronage about the relationships.

DIANA, PRINCESS OF WALES

The late Diana, Princess of Wales was by far the most popular member of the Royal Family to the public during her lifetime, but not always to her staff. She could be the most loved and adored and occasionally the most disliked and feared when her mood changed. Generous to a fault, she encouraged familiarity with her staff, even joining her chef in the kitchen at Kensington Palace where she would sit on the table, swinging her legs and enjoying a good gossip. She would often ask for egg and chips to be served with lashings of ketchup. The next day she could be the most imperious of women; a regular prima donna; demanding, suspicious and autocratic. She inspired devotion more than fear. But the staff never quite knew where they were with her – and royal servants like to know their place, and for their masters and mistresses to know theirs. It's safer that way. One of her staff said Diana was very easy to love, but not so easy to like.

Several of her protection officers asked to be moved because of her capricious behaviour and Oliver Everett, one of the most trusted officials in the Royal

Household, was charged with instructing Diana, before she became Princess of Wales, in how to walk down the aisle at her wedding. He did this by attaching pieces of paper to an ordinary day dress to simulate the twenty-five foot train on the actual wedding dress. Oliver and Diana got along famously, until shortly after the wedding, when, once again, he found it difficult to cope with her moods. He resigned from the Household of the Prince and Princess of Wales, and found himself working for The Queen as Librarian at Windsor Castle. So it wasn't all sweetness and light with the woman who was regarded by many as the most adored person in the world.

THE DUKE OF EDINBURGH

Prince Philip, who receives £359,000 a year from Government funds to meet his public duty expenses, has always had a reputation for being rude and overbearing, but excluding The Queen's personal staff, he employs the most loyal team anywhere in the Household. They will not hear a word said against their boss, and even though he still rants and raves from time to time, he doesn't bear grudges, so they all know that once he has got something off his chest, even when it means they have to stand and take the most appalling abuse, he will forget it the following day – as if nothing has happened.

The present author was once sitting in the office of Sir Philip [later Lord] Moore, private secretary to The Queen, when Prince Philip burst in and proceeded to give the poor man the most horrific verbal roasting. All the while Sir Philip (a man who had been a gallant Bomber Command pilot during the Second World War and later played rugby for England) stood there and did not say a word. When Prince Philip left, Sir Philip apologised to me for having to witness the incident and then mentioned that the matter that HRH was accusing him of was, in fact, the responsibility of someone else. When I asked why on earth he didn't speak up for himself, he replied, 'You have to remember, in this house, royalty may not always be right, but they are never wrong.'

Apparently, later in the day, the Duke of Edinburgh spoke to Sir Philip as if the row had never occurred. It was just a normal glitch in the average day at Buckingham Palace. But if the situation had been reversed, Philip Moore would have been out of the Palace without his feet touching the ground.

But there is one characteristic that endears Prince Philip to his staff. His loyalty to them is second to none; unlike some other members of the family to whom loyalty is a one-way street. Philip will go out of his way to protect any of his team, from his valets to his most senior private secretary, if he believes they are in the right. There is a large turnover of staff in certain offices, but Prince Philip's team are the longest serving of any – including that of Her Majesty. And when his chauffeur died in 2011, Prince Philip did not send a representative to the funeral, he broke with tradition by insisting on attending himself, showing how high a regard he had for the man who had served him loyally for many years.

Prince Philip is a man who had to endure humiliation the moment he joined the Royal Family. His
father-in-law, King George VI grudgingly granted him
the right to be styled His Royal Highness the Duke of
Edinburgh, on his marriage to Princess Elizabeth in
1947, but refused to permit him to be called a Prince,
even though he had previously been Prince Philip of
Greece and at the time of his birth he was sixth in line
to the Greek throne. So in some ways he was more
royal than his wife, as she had a mother who had been
born a commoner.

It was when Princess Elizabeth became Queen that
she made up for her father's attitude and showered
honours on Philip, creating him a Prince of the United
Kingdom in 1957; Knight of the Garter; Knight of the
Thistle; awarding him the Order of Merit and making
him a Privy Councillor. So in effect, every honour that
Prince Phillip has received has been from his wife.

While The Queen wears the crown, in the
Mountbatten/Windsor family there is no doubt that
Philip wears the trousers. Even at his great age, he still
summons his four children to Balmoral every year –
without The Queen present – even though they have
all married and had children of their own.

He carries out a review of the previous year: what
they have achieved; their successes and their failures.
He doesn't pull his punches, but neither is he unfair
and if one of them disagrees with his assessment, he
will listen to their arguments. He accepts reasons but
not excuses.

In the early days it was a bit like being hauled in
front of the headmaster; these days it's more of a family

debate. If there is one major family disappointment it is Philip's relationship with his eldest son who he believes is indecisive. Prince Philip has definite views on everything; he is ambivalent about nothing; just like his daughter Anne.

Of course, where The Queen is forced to steer clear of anything controversial, her husband appears to court it deliberately. He favours the head-on approach. Where she is required not to voice her opinions in public, there are no such constitutional constraints on Philip. He also likes to provoke argument with those who might be regarded as his social inferiors. One day he met an attractive young woman in the corridors of Buckingham Palace. Not recognising her, he asked what she was doing there and where she worked. She replied that she was employed in the Royal Collection. To which he said, 'They are all mad there.' She was then quick-witted enough to come back with the words 'Yes, Sir. It's one of the prime qualifications'. He was greatly amused and later told The Queen about the encounter.

PRINCESS MARGARET

Second in the popularity league table was the late Princess Margaret, The Queen's only sister, who died in 2002. She lived in great splendour in a thirty-five-room apartment at 1A Clock Court in Kensington Palace, a home that for years was the centre of society among stars of show business, films and the arts. Margaret was acknowledged, even within her own family, as the most Regal and arrogant of them all. She would never allow anyone, for an instant, to forget who she was and the position she occupied. She would not speak directly on the telephone to anyone unless they were of equal or higher rank, which narrowed the field down quite a bit. All others were instructed to speak to an aide and relay messages to her.

A young Welsh Guards officer was invited by a mutual friend to join the Princess at a dinner party. This was late in 1951 when the world knew that her father, King George VI, was seriously ill. The young officer was seated next to Margaret and when he was presented to her he politely asked how her father was feeling. 'Are you referring to His *Majesty*?' she frostily replied and then pointedly ignored him for the remainder of the evening.

On a later occasion, the wife of one of the Household private secretaries was on the guest list at a dinner party. This lady was from the Argentine and this was at the time of the Falklands conflict. When the Princess, who was seated near the guest, tried to guess at her accent, and failed, she eventually demanded to know where she had come from. On being told it was the Argentine, she turned her back and not only ignored her for the rest of the evening but excluded her from the conversation until the meal was over. It was an example of the extreme bad manners that Margaret would display on many occasions. Which makes it surprising that she was a popular employer among Palace staff.

One of her former police protection officers said that when he was told he was going to work for her, his heart sank because of her reputation as a tyrant. However, the reverse was true. The first thing Margaret showed him was how she liked her drinks mixed. Her favourite was The Famous Grouse whisky, poured over ice cubes, with a little soda water added. She explained the exact measurements and told him that as long as he got it right every time they would get along famously. But the first time he got it wrong, he would be out on his ear. He must have done something right as he continued to work for her quite happily until he was moved to a younger member of the Royal Family.

When Margaret and Lord Snowdon were married, his valet, and other male servants, would frequently walk into the Princess's dressing room to find her sitting at her dressing table stark naked. She didn't bat an eyelid or try to cover herself. It was as if they didn't even exist – just another piece of furniture. But, again, like her brother-in-law, Prince Philip, Margaret could be extremely loyal and if she found out that one of her staff was in trouble, she would go to bat for them. She was also generous to a fault. When she found out that the wife of one of her chefs needed surgery, she arranged for the woman to go into a private hospital immediately and paid all the bills herself. At Christmastime, her staff would all be treated to a slap-up meal at an expensive restaurant – but she declined to join them. Democracy went only so far.

There was one occasion though when Princess Margaret found herself upstaged by one of her maids. A young woman had been employed on a temporary basis, and one of the ways in which she liked to amuse herself, when Princess Margaret was out, was to try on her clothes, as they had the same measurements. She took this a step further one evening when she had been invited out to an expensive restaurant by a new admirer. She 'borrowed' one of Margaret's favourite dresses, knowing she would be back before the boss and no one would know. How wrong she was. By a chance in million, Margaret was dining at the same restaurant that evening and saw the girl – and the frock. Neither acknowledged the other but the following morning the maid was summoned and informed her 'temporary' employment would not be made permanent. In fact it was terminated that very day. However, the Princess did not appear to mind too much the fact that her maid had worn one of her dresses; she wanted to know how the girl and her companion could afford to eat at the same restaurant where she was dining. No explanation was forthcoming – and Margaret continued to wear the dress.

(The Queen's clothes are a source of constant comment in the media and she will wear a favourite outfit for years. When she finally tires of it, she will hand it to one of her dressers, who can either wear it or sell it, with one proviso, all labels must be removed and anything that could possibly identify it as having come from royalty obliterated. One frock found it's way to a jumble sale near Sandringham, but in spite of its obvious quality, it failed to sell.)

The late Sir Harry Secombe and his wife Myra knew Princess Margaret through their mutual friend, Peter Sellers. On one occasion, the Secombes were staying at their holiday home in Majorca and were preparing to leave, having packed all their belongings except for the clothes they intended to wear for the flight home.

Princess Margaret was on vacation nearby with friends and she sent one of her ladies-in-waiting over to invite them to join her for dinner. They immediately unpacked and dressed in their finery, only to find when they arrived, that the Princess and her friends were all in swimsuits. Margaret thought it was hilarious and luckily, Harry, who could see a joke in anything, turned it to his and Myra's advantage and at one point he went inside, stripped to his shorts and returned wearing just that and his bow tie. Turning to Princess Margaret, he said, 'Well, it did say, black tie.' Whereupon she had to admit defeat. Which, to be fair, she did with plenty of grace.

THE PRINCESS ROYAL

The third most popular person in the employment stakes is the Princess Royal, who is paid £228,000 a year to offset the cost of her office and official duties. The Queen's only daughter is notorious for her frugality, in a family where such a description is regarded as a great compliment. While her brother, Charles, could not survive without the ministrations of nearly a hundred staff, Anne manages with the service of just three: a cook, cleaner and a lady-in-waiting who doubles as office administrator at Gatcombe Park, the Princess's home in Gloucestershire.

Anne used to employ a butler, who rarely dressed in the traditional garb of tailcoat and striped trousers.

He was usually seen around the place wearing a check shirt and corduroy trousers held up with a frayed belt. He was handy to have around the place when Peter and Zara, Anne's children were younger, but once they had grown up and left home, she realised he didn't have too much to do and he was eating and drinking more than he was worth so she dispensed with his services. She is able to call on temporary staff when the occasion demands such as a dinner party, when Anne is the perfect hostess and Gatcombe looks every inch a royal residence.

The house is very easy to miss if you haven't been there before. Situated at the end of a long lane, there is no nameplate to indicate Gatcombe or who lives there. The main house is half a mile along the drive and it suddenly divides into two with a signpost directing visitors towards the right. This takes you around the back of the property, past a police post that has been so skilfully built it blends into the surrounding woodland and is barely noticeable. Policemen from the Gloucestershire force man the post 24/7. If you are expected, and all others do not get past the police post, you will be allowed to drive towards the front of the house and park on the gravel.

Gatcombe Park stands in 1,200 acres of superb Gloucestershire countryside. It was built from 1771 to 1774 by Edward Sheppard, a wealthy sheep breeder and wool merchant and the property changed hands many times until, in 1940, it was bought by Samuel Courtauld, a mega-rich textile manufacturer, whose son-in-law was the late Lord (Rab) Butler, a prominent Conservative Member of Parliament in the

1950s and 1960s, who rose to Cabinet rank, and was once referred to as the best Prime Minister Britain never had.

Gatcombe hadn't been lived in for more than ten years and it was in a dilapidated state of repair with no rooms ready to move in to, when Butler suggested that Princess Anne and Mark Phillips might find it suitable, mainly because they were looking for somewhere with equestrian facilities.

The price was a bit daunting (originally it was £700,000) and Mark's army salary of £4,000 a year wouldn't have covered even the interest payments on the mortgage. Which is when The Queen stepped in and bought it, with a £200,000 reduction on the asking price. It was an astute investment as the estate is now valued at over £5 million.

When the news of the purchase became public there was the expected amount of criticism. Why did two young people need such a property? Neil Kinnock, before he became Leader of the Labour Party and long before he was ennobled as Lord Kinnock, said, 'I don't know which is worse – The Queen for being wealthy enough to give it to them, or them [sic] for having the neck to take it.' (In later years, Neil Kinnock and his wife, Glenys, were overnight guests of The Queen at Windsor Castle and afterwards said they thoroughly enjoyed the experience.)

But as with other property deals involving The Queen, the house was not put in the couple's name, just in case there was a divorce, which of course, duly happened. Similarly, when Princess Margaret and Lord Snowdon divorced, The Queen bought her former brother-in-law a house in Kensington for around £70,000 (worth an estimated £5 million today). But the property was put in the names of her nephew and niece, Viscount Linley and Lady Sarah Chatto, the couple's children. As Lord Snowdon later remarried, and divorced, it was a sensible measure to protect the children's legacy. The Queen had already taken steps to protect her oldest grandchildren from any possible future financial difficulties from the moment they were born. Peter and Zara Phillips are the beneficiaries of large trust funds established on their behalf by Her Majesty. The funds, £1 million each when they were born, have grown through judicious investment, so that today they are worth three times the original amount. Zara and Mike Tindall, the England rugby international she married in July 2011, were able to buy an £800,000 house in Cheltenham, with presumably no problem raising a mortgage, having lived together for some years in a house on the Gatcombe estate, provided for them by Princess Anne. Zara's equestrian earnings (she is a former World and European Three-Day Event Champion) plus lucrative sponsorships and Mike's six-figure contract with Gloucester, means they are both in the higher tax-paying bracket. Zara's trustees include two of her mother's oldest friends, Brigadier Andrew Parker Bowles and the former world champion Formula One racing driver, Sir Jackie Stewart, whose business acumen has been one of the main reasons for the trust's growth. Sir Jackie, and his wife Helen, who is Godmother to Zara, have known the Princess Royal since Jackie shared the Sports Personality of the Year award with Anne in 1971.

Gatcombe Park itself is not as large as it looks in pictures, mainly because of the huge conservatory that was added in 1829, making the place look enormous. In reality, it is a fairly modest country mansion. Certainly not a stately home by any means. There are thirty-two rooms in all, with a formal drawing room on the left, as you go in, leading to the Princess's sitting room, where she likes to work on her speeches and deals with correspondence. On the other side of the hall is the dining room – rarely used as such, and only when a dinner party is held. Otherwise it contains piles of books and magazines, stacked on the table. Beyond the dining room is the study. This is a comfortable retreat with deep armchairs and a television set, a large desk and two telephones. The kitchen is on the ground floor with the bedrooms on the first floor with the master bedroom commanding spectacular views over the valley in front of the house. Above the principal bedrooms is what used to be the nursery suite with its own kitchen and bathrooms. But this is no longer required as the children have long since left home. So now it is available for staff or any visitors who cannot be accommodated on the floor beneath.

Visitors often remark on how informal life appears to be at Gatcombe, but, as one of her former police officers said, appearances can be deceptive and you take the outward signs of informality at your peril if you work there. No one confuses Anne's apparent friendliness as a sign that one can become familiar. And nobody, even within the family, has ever heard her addressed, or referred to, as 'Annie'.

Having said that, her staff remain with her for years because, they say, they always know where they are with her. She is not moody or sulky, but neither is she outgoing. They all know that early mornings are not her best time so they keep out of her way and if she is working – which is what happens most days – she may not even return a 'good morning' greeting, as her mind is on the programme ahead and she is concentrating.

One way in which her team can recognise if they are part of the inner circle is if she makes a joke at their expense. There was a youngish member of the staff with a receding hairline, and on one occasion they had witnessed something that both amused and slightly shocked her. Turning to him she said, 'It's enough to make your hair stand on end.' Then looking up at his balding pate she added, 'Well, perhaps not in your case.'

She was actually paying him a backhanded compliment. If he had been a stranger, or someone new to her, she would not have dreamt of saying something so personal; she has impeccable manners when dealing with outsiders. He took it in the spirit it was intended and they both had a good laugh.

But had the positions been reversed she would certainly not have seen the joke. They all know it doesn't pay to try and be clever with the boss.

One of her early private secretaries discovered to his cost that it was not the done thing to speak out of turn. During a car journey, he uttered an opinion that she took as a personal criticism. What he said was that he thought he had been in the job long enough and was considering resigning. Taking it as a slight upon herself, she ignored him for the rest of the journey. He was obviously right to feel he had outstayed his welcome as he resigned straight away – and he is no longer on her Christmas card list.

The lynchpin of the Household at Gatcombe is a lady-in-waiting who actually controls the day-to-day logistics at the country house (Nick Wright, a genial and highly efficient former Royal Navy Captain, is Private Secretary based at Buckingham Palace with a small office staff of five, from where he handles all enquiries regarding the official programme). The lady at Gatcombe, who acts as a personal secretary, is an invaluable conduit as she is able to tell Nick Wright and the other ladies-in-waiting and police officers on duty about the Princess's state of mind on any particular day, so they know in advance how to approach her, and when to keep quiet.

Mark Phillips, the Princess's first husband was well liked by his wife's staff. His easy-going, laid-back manner made him a pleasant, undemanding consort and today, since their divorce, he remains on excellent terms with everyone. He lives at Aston Farm – leased from The Queen – next door to Gatcombe and still organises commercial shooting parties with the Princess throughout the season. Peter and Zara adore their father; their relationship with their stepfather, Tim Laurence, is correct if not entirely cordial and is said to be maintained mainly for the sake of their mother.

Admiral Laurence, who recently retired from the Royal Navy to take up a well-paid position in the private sector, is not held in the highest regard by staff at Buckingham Palace. He is thought of as a man with ideas way beyond his station and who has also, on occasion, adopted attitudes, not usually found among those born to the purple.

An example of the Princess Royal's loyalty to her staff occurred when the late Lt Col. Peter Gibbs, who had been her Private Secretary for eighteen years, the longest serving of any of her servants, retired on reaching the mandatory age. Without telling him, she arranged for Col. Gibbs to be received by The Queen on his final day. When he entered Her Majesty's sitting room he saw a kneeling stool in the centre of the room and imagined it was for someone coming after him. However, The Queen then knighted him for his long and distinguished service and he emerged as Sir Peter Gibbs, KCVO. It was a thoughtful and generous gesture on the Princess's part and no one was more surprised than Peter himself.

If there is one thing that distinguishes her from her brother Charles, it is her decisiveness. Where Prince Charles has been known to change his mind and his opinions in the blink of an eye, indecisiveness is not a word in Anne's vocabulary. As one of her private secretaries remarked, 'the difficulty is getting her to change her mind once she's decided. She may be wrong in some of the decisions she takes but at least they are her own decisions, and not based on the opinions of the last person she has spoken to.'

Her staff sometimes despair of getting her to see their point of view, which is why they tread very carefully around her. But they know that if they are blamed for something that is clearly not their fault, they can rely on her to back them up – which is why she comes so high in the list of popular employers.

Where once her image was that of an uncooperative, aggressive and surly young Princess, she has developed over the years into a thoroughly dependable, mature woman whose knowledge and professionalism as a working royal is unparalleled. And nobody appreciates the Princess Royal more than her parents. To The Queen and Prince Philip she has been a willing and enthusiastic member of 'The Firm' for over forty years, and they are delighted that there is no sign of her reducing her commitments in the near future.

THE PRINCE OF WALES

The Prince of Wales has the largest Household other than The Queen and also, at Clarence House, the highest turnover of staff, with the majority of the 'pre-Diana' servants having left or been quietly 'let go', it is hinted at the suggestion of the Duchess of Cornwall.

When Prince Charles comes from an engagement, whether it's a royal duty in London, or one of his sporting activities in the country – fishing and shooting in Scotland, shooting again at Sandringham or riding at his country home in Gloucestershire – he always changes his outfits, dropping on the floor whatever he is wearing at the time.

Prince Charles has never known what it is to have to pick up his own clothes once he has undressed or changed, choose which of his 100 suits to wear, decide which shirt or tie to put on, or clean his own shoes – an orderly from the Welsh Guards arrives at Clarence House from nearby Wellington Barracks and performs this task every day. When His Royal Highness leaves for one of his many journeys, either abroad or in Britain, someone else does the packing and unpacking, arranges the transport and makes sure he arrives at the correct place at the appointed hour. His chef selects his meals, with all his bills being paid by a man who goes by the exalted title of Treasurer to HRH's Household.

One of the Prince's three valets makes sure his bath has been run, with the water temperature tested with a wooden-cased thermometer, that a fresh blade is inserted in his razor before he shaves each morning and also included in his duties is the task of squeezing three quarters, no more, no less, of an inch of tooth-paste onto the royal toothbrush.

Like almost all the Royal Family, Prince Charles hates confrontation, even with servants, and legend has it that on one occasion his then valet Stephen Barry received a handwritten note complaining that Stephen knew the Prince was right-handed, so why had he left the toothbrush that morning with the handle facing left. Barry thought there was nothing unusual in seeing this note and made sure it didn't happen again.

Prince Charles is an ideal employer, as long as everything is perfect.

On another occasion, the Prince found three ties laid out when he was getting dressed. He asked his valet what they were for and was told that the serv-ant thought he might like to select which one to wear.

Charles reprimanded the man, telling him that he should choose, which is what he was paid to do. As the Prince often has a number of engagements in London on the same day without time to return to Clarence House, his valet will place a number of different ties in the car so his master can change en route. If Charles is visiting different organisations or military establishments with which he is associated, he pays them the compliment of wearing their tie. The record for one day is, apparently, five different ties.

His personal staff, such as valets, who are closer to him than anyone, are treated extremely well. They all usually start off as footmen in the Palace and when they are promoted to work directly for the Heir to the Throne their living conditions and salary improves considerably. They are housed in rooms near to their principal's, so they are on hand when he rings for them, and they no longer have to wear livery, but are sent to one of HRH's tailors to be measured for a number of suits – at his expense. His valets all wear dark grey or navy blue suits, except when they act as loaders when he goes shooting. Then they are clad in sporting clothes, again hand-tailored, with the jackets in Balmoral tartan – and they are given instructions in how to load his shotguns at Purdeys, the royal gunsmiths. Their suits are made by one of London's leading tailors and the valets (to all the royal men) have in the past sometimes been offered little 'inducements' to recommend them: an extra pair of trousers in a different pattern or a sports jacket. One even managed to obtain a brand new evening suit that he said was nicer than his boss's.

One important lesson the Prince of Wales's valets have to learn is the correct way to dress their master in one of his many uniforms: military, naval and Royal Air Force, and also the proper order in which his decorations should be worn. The Queen and the Duke of Edinburgh are believed to quietly disapprove of their eldest son's ostentatious lifestyle. He lives in a far grander manner than they enjoy, with Clarence House, said to be the most elegant council house in Britain, maintaining standards few other houses in Britain are able to sustain today.

Of course, as with Buckingham Palace, Clarence House is not merely the London home of the Prince of Wales and the Duchess of Cornwall. It is also the centre of an enormous business undertaking, with the Prince's links with his hundreds of charities need-ing office space. So much so that his staff, including the Prince's Trust, has expanded to take over a large number of rooms in St James's Palace, across Stable Yard, much to the annoyance of the Royal Collection who have been forced to abandon their own expansion plans for the building.

New staff at Clarence House – and it applies to Highgrove in Gloucestershire and Birkhall in Balmoral, where a skeleton staff remains throughout the year with the main body moving with the royal couple as and when required – rapidly learn their boss's idiosyncrasies. He hates waste, calling it his 'Scottish meanness' and has been known in the past to check the contents of the larder and fridge to make sure he is not being overcharged. Food is not one of his great passions however. He prefers simple dishes;

school food really. He drinks tea in the afternoon, but unlike his father, does not care for coffee and no one can recall him ever drinking a cup.

The housemaids who work for the Prince and Duchess have a difficult task in keeping their rooms dust free. They collect so much of what the maids call junk that the rooms are dust traps and take hours to clean. And the Prince seems to know every item, where it came from, who gave it, and where its proper place is. So if one is missing, he will not rest until it's found.

His valets are expert in knowing how to tie their master's shoelaces. Some have to be cross-stitched and others simply tied straight, depending on which pair of shoes he is going to wear. And all laces have to be ironed whenever the shoes are taken off.

The valets keep a checklist of the outfits worn on a particular day, and where, so they can tell their principal if he has worn something to the same place on more than one occasion.

They also need to be taught how to recognise the different uniforms the Prince wears. Like his father, the Duke of Edinburgh, Prince Charles has over forty uniforms: Army, Royal Navy, Royal Air Force, plus tropical kit for his overseas tours. The valets are meticulous in making sure his decorations are placed in the correct order. His Royal Highness has an encyclopaedic knowledge of military medals and notices if one is even slightly out of place. And even if he didn't, The Queen would quickly point it out. His knowledge is exceeded only by hers.

The Prince of Wales's staff are kept on their toes as he has only one standard – perfection. He is a temperamental man, given to introspection, and among the Royal Family he is considered to be the most indecisive member. Charles was once said to always reflect the views of the last person he had spoken to, which is not entirely fair, as he does have definite opinions of his own. However, his staff, and that includes not only the domestics but also his large secretarial team, never quite know where they stand with him. One day he will be friendly and talkative, the next distant and aloof. And, as was previously stated, as he avoids direct confrontation, it is often unclear to someone whether they have done something wrong, or indeed what that might be. The only way they can tell if they have fallen out of favour is if there is a slight cooling towards them in his manner.

However, his staff tend to remain loyal and in his service for years, so obviously he is popular as an employer. And, in spite of the 'Scottish meanness' he is among the most generous of the Royal Family. No one has cause to complain about their living and working conditions and he pays well above the going rate to everyone from his Private Secretary down to the most junior housemaids and footmen.

The Prince is kept informed by his staff of the comings and goings of anyone in whom they think he might have an interest. Recently, he was told that a former royal correspondent for a national newspaper, who had frequently attacked him in print, had undergone surgery for a serious stomach condition. The former reporter was surprised – and delighted – when a large and very expensive bunch of his favourite flowers were delivered to his home, along with a handwritten note from his old adversary wishing him well. It was a generous and thoughtful gesture that was entirely spontaneous, and, on his orders, carried out without any publicity.

THE DUCHESS OF CORNWALL

The Duchess of Cornwall is not as universally liked as her husband, but her small personal staff is loyal and will not hear a word said against her. Even if privately some of them may have reservations.

The attention to detail the Royals insist upon is remarkable in this day and age. For instance, Camilla, Duchess of Cornwall, likes to smoke, so footmen at all the homes she shares with Prince Charles are instructed to place silver cigarette boxes containing her favourite brand in every room, and also to make sure that matchbox holders in solid silver containers are placed upright near at hand with one match half withdrawn so she does not have to scrabble about looking for a light. The moment she leaves a room – even if it just for a few minutes – a footman makes sure the ashtrays are emptied, ready for her return. Her cigarette bill is said to come to over £100 a week. It's the only extravagance Prince Charles is believed to object to regarding his wife's expenses. A lifelong opponent of smoking, the Prince has tried to persuade her to give up, without success. But at least she has cut down in recent years. The Duchess never smokes at Buckingham Palace, where there is a strict no-smoking policy.

If there is one aspect of working for the Prince of Wales and his wife that the domestic staff do not enjoy it is that they have to spend part of their time at Highgrove House on the outskirts of the pleasant if sleepy market town of Tetbury. The Prince always likes to claim he is not a city person and much prefers to live in the country. The staff prefer the bright lights of London. When they are off-duty at Highgrove, the only entertainment they can find is in one of the local pubs. Tetbury is the sort of town where everything closes down at eleven. Highgrove is a nine-bedroomed Georgian mansion, which was bought for the Prince by his Duchy of Cornwall. When it was first bought, the estate comprised of 350 acres and it has since been extended considerably. It belonged to the late Maurice Macmillan, son of the former Prime Minister, Harold Macmillan, later Earl of Stockton, for the bargain price of £800,000. Today it is estimated to be worth well over £10 million, partly of course because of its royal provenance. The presence of royalty has been reflected in property prices in the area, with at least a couple of zeros being added to selling prices since the Prince of Wales moved in.

In addition to the nine principal bedrooms at Highgrove, there are six bathrooms, four elegant reception rooms and a swimming pool, plus one other unusual feature for an English country house: a steel-lined room, which is said to be impregnable in the event of attack by terrorists. It is on the first floor and though constructed of steel it is called by the Household the Iron Room. It is tiny, just 20ft x 20ft, and has been so built that even if the rest of the house is destroyed, it will drop intact to the ground floor. Inside are medical supplies, including containers of Charles and Camilla's blood group, long-lasting food and drinks, an armoury, radio transmitters equipped to obtain a signal even within its steel walls, air purifiers and chemical lavatories. The royal couple could, if necessary, survive for weeks – even if it might be a little cramped.

The Iron Room is one part of Highgrove that is not shown to visitors.

The garden is Prince Charles's pride and joy and he takes immense pleasure in showing groups of fellow enthusiasts his plants, shrubs and flowers. There is also a Home Farm where his now-famous Duchy Originals are grown and which add considerably to the Duchy's profits.

Prince Charles's brothers, Andrew and Edward, do not enjoy anywhere as lavish a lifestyle, but they do not stint themselves in any way.

The Duke of York

Prince Andrew, the Duke of York, is the second highest paid member of the Royal Family, receiving £249,000 a year for his official expenses. He inherited the lease of Royal Lodge in Windsor Great Park, from his grandmother, the late Queen Elizabeth, The Queen Mother. The house lies halfway between Windsor Castle and Virginia Water, towards the eastern side of Windsor Great Park. The Queen Mother died in 2002 and Andrew took over the lease from the Crown Estates in

2004 after spending more than £7.5 million on renovations for the thirty-room Grade II-listed property, which included building a brand new indoor swimming pool. The rent for the house and forty-hectare grounds is a little over £15,000 a year – or £250 a week, which Andrew was perfectly able to afford, having sold his nearby house Sunninghill Park (which is said to be now in ruins) for a reported £15 million, some £3 million over the original asking price. Added to which he receives a Royal Navy pension of approximately £17,000 a year plus £249,000 a year from the Civil List, which, in fairness, is not a salary, but which goes towards the expenditure on his public duties.

It was in 1931 that the then Duke of York, second son of King George V, asked his father if he and his wife could have the house and they were given the lease as a 'Grace and Favour' home. The Duchess (later The Queen Mother) loved the place so much that when her husband (as King George VI) died in 1952, she continued to use the property at weekends for the rest of her life.

The house has unusual proportions, being dominated by the Saloon, which is forty-eight feet long, twenty-nine feet wide and twenty feet high, entirely suitable for the sort of parties that the present Duke of York likes to throw when his guests include a number of fabulously wealthy Middle-Eastern friends. The décor that His Royal Highness favours also reflects some of the tastes of his friends, though his servants, who privately are appalled, do not share it.

The gardens at Royal Lodge are among the finest of any enjoyed by Andrew's siblings and consist mainly of woodland and immaculate lawns. There is also an outdoor swimming pool, enjoyed by his daughters Beatrice and Eugenie and also Andrew's ex-wife, Sarah, Duchess of York, who although they have been divorced for years, remains on excellent terms with her ex and shares Royal Lodge whenever she is in England. Theirs is among the most civilised divorces one can imagine. No animosity, just mutual affection. They just cannot live together permanently.

When Fergie is staying at Royal Lodge, the staff enjoy her company. She makes the party go with a swing and there is a warm atmosphere that affects everyone from Andrew down to the staff in the kitchens. Her demands are few, unlike her ex-husband who can be difficult in the extreme. His staff move around him with caution as his occasionally boorish behaviour, childish tantrums and his mood swings means they never quite know what to expect.

Unusually, considering his reputation, Prince Andrew does not object to senior members of the Household hosting functions in the Salon of Royal Lodge, as long as he doesn't have to be present. One of the more recent occurred in June 2011 during Royal Ascot Week when a luncheon party was being held (Andrew was at lunch at Windsor Castle). Everything was going with a swing, when suddenly Princess Beatrice entered the room unannounced. The guests were not too sure how to react; after all this was her home, but she was in excellent form, moving among them, chatting informally and making them all feel they were welcome. It was a pleasant gesture in complete contrast to the unfortunate publicity that

Beatrice and her sister Eugenie had received following their disastrous appearance at the wedding of William and Catherine. It was the icing on the cake and made for a wonderful interlude before they left for the races.

THE EARL OF WESSEX

The baby brother of the Royal Family, Prince Edward, Earl of Wessex, with an estimated wealth of £9 million, and an income of £141,000 a year from Government funds, lives in one of the grandest houses, Bagshot Park, with a full retinue of liveried servants and gardeners to look after the extensive grounds. The Countess has recently upset neighbours by asking the local authority to close certain rights of way that criss-cross the Bagshot estate. She claims that it makes it far too easy for intruders to get in or for walkers to wander into their garden.

Bagshot Park has a long royal pedigree having been built originally for King Charles I as one of his many hunting lodges. Since then many subsequent members of royalty have lived there with the last, before Prince Edward took it over, being Prince Arthur, Duke of Connaught, a son of Queen Victoria, who died at Bagshot in 1942.

The present house is situated in grounds of eighty-eight acres and contains fifty-six rooms, making it at least three times bigger than Highgrove, the country home of the Prince of Wales. The annual running costs are around £250,000, with Edward paying the princely sum of less than £200 a week in rent, after sub-letting a converted stable block for £80,000 a year to a pharmaceutical company. No one would blame him for displaying such business acumen, but the fact that he alone was offered the fifty-year lease on the property led to accusations in Parliament that the Royal Family was receiving preferential treatment by the Crown Estates. If both Royal Lodge and/or Bagshot Park were placed on the open market, the former would fetch up to £20,000 a week in rent, while Bagshot Park is currently reckoned to be worth around £25 million. The Crown Estates claim that the reason they chose the two Princes as tenants is because of the security precautions necessary in such a sensitive area so close to The Queen at Windsor Castle.

The Household at Bagshot Park is formal and correct, which is the way both sides of the green baize door prefer it. Each one knows exactly what they should do and how they should behave.

Prince Edward does not allow any of his servants to get too close, unlike Prince Charles, whose personal staff are made to feel they are friends – so long as they remember who is boss and who is servant.

Prince Edward is considered by the Household to be the most pompous member of the Royal Family, insisting on absolute formality at all times. He once was said to have reprimanded a butler because the man was not outside the house when he arrived back and Edward had to open the car door himself. His chauffeur is instructed to face the front at all times, even when the car is stationary, as are the police officers who protect the Earl and Countess. Edward even had his policemen given instruction by Swaine, Adeney,

Brigg & Son, the royal suppliers of whips, gloves and umbrellas, on how to correctly furl an umbrella. Apparently, one holds the tip in the left hand with the handle in the right, and then slowly brings the hand down 'brolly' holding it as tight as possible while turning the handle in the opposite direction.

Edward addresses his police officers, pages, chauffeurs by their surname. Younger staff: footmen, valets and housemaids are called by their Christian names. This is a system used by most members of the Royal Family; one former police officer, who had served The Queen for over twenty years without once being addressed by his Christian name, was invited to shoot with the Duke of Edinburgh at Balmoral when he retired. He said the only difference was that, as a guest, The Queen and Prince Philip used his Christian name.

Prince Edward is aloof and distant but, contrary to his public image, he can be helpful towards outsiders who arrive at his home to carry out a task. A well-known photographer drove her car to Bagshot to take some pictures of the children. When she arrived, the butler saw her struggling with her equipment but made no move to help. Then Prince Edward came out, saw the situation and immediately picked up her tripod, put it on his shoulder and carried it inside the house. No other member of the Royal Family would dream of assisting in this way. So perhaps his so-called aloofness is actually shyness.

The Countess of Wessex, Sophie, is a great favourite of The Queen, but staff are wary when dealing with her as she can become rather aware of her position on occasion, forgetting that she is only royal by marriage, not birth. She has also become more figure-conscious since the former Catherine Middleton, now the Duchess of Cambridge, joined the royal firm. After seeing the svelte, slim-line Duchess at the Royal Wedding and stealing the show at Royal Ascot, Sophie Wessex decided she too needed to pay attention to her own figure; not that she is overweight by any means. She hired a personal trainer, who visits her every morning at Bagshot Park and together they work out in the grounds.

The Earl of Wessex is fascinated by his family's background and his enquiring mind has discovered a few interesting facts about the house he now occupies.

In 1881, the house staff records show that twenty-six servants lived in the main house (it was a much larger property then with 120 rooms). There was an under butler, a housekeeper, four valets, two lady's maids, two dressers, a cook, three kitchen maids, three housemaids, three footmen, a page, a porter, a scullery maid (now they call them kitchen operatives) and a serving soldier. Outside the main house a coachman and seven grooms lived in the Mews, three agricultural workers and two further domestics lived in lodges with a gardener completing the staff. It's not quite like that today, but the current tenant of Bagshot Park, with a mere fifty-six rooms, manages to exist with less than a quarter of the number of staff his oldest brother employs.

Both the brothers, Andrew and Edward (and other members of the Royal Family) keep small notebooks handy to make comments about service and food and drink. Remarks such as: 'Red wine not allowed to breathe long enough,' and 'White wine could have been chilled a little more.' Or, 'Remind footman to place spoons a little closer to the plate.' This is so they will not have to stretch to reach them. Experienced servants take these sorts of comments in their stride. They know that if there is a serious complaint, they always have the Civil Service Union, to which they now all belong, behind them. Even though, as members of the Royal Household, they do not have to strike when other union members act. There is a special exemption for The Queen's staff. The domestic servants also like to have a joke at the expense of the Royals when they can. Occasionally one will hear a couple of footmen chatting in 'cut-glass' accents about whether 'the Lager has been allowed to breathe long enough' and 'has it been decanted correctly'. The younger men enjoy this sort of parody, just as long as the Palace Steward doesn't hear them. He is not the sort of man to permit any levity about members of the Royal Family.

THE GLOUCESTERS AND KENTS

In the Order of Precedence, the Duke and Duchess of Gloucester are higher than their cousins the Duke and Duchess of Kent, but as the Duke of Kent undertakes more public duties (the Duchess no longer plays a part in public life), he receives the larger annuity of £236,000. The Duke and Duchess of Gloucester, who both are involved in royal duties, receive £175,000 a year.

Their servants and their protection officers generally like the 'second division' of the Royal Family, the Gloucesters and Kents. They are not too demanding and are probably among the most democratic of the Royals. The Duke of Kent in particular gets on well with everyone and one of his staff tells the story of how his boss even tried to give way when they were both trying to grab the same taxi.

The Duke was late for an appointment leaving his apartment, at that time in St James's Palace – this was in the days when junior royalty could move freely without the ever-present armed bodyguards – and, seeing a taxi coming along Pall Mall towards St James's Street he ran and waved it down, not noticing that someone else was approaching from the other side. They arrived at the cab at the same time and His Royal Highness, without recognising the man, displayed his usual perfect manners and stood back. When their eyes met, both realised who the other was. The servant bowed to the Duke and apologised. Whereupon the Duke insisted that his man had been there first. Then he asked where the servant was going. On being told he was heading towards Paddington, which is where he too was going, he suggested they share the taxi, which they did, and when they arrived he insisted on paying, waving away his fellow passenger's offer to pay his share. It is difficult, if not impossible, to imagine any other member of the Royal Family, of whatever status or rank, behaving in such a manner.

The Duchess of Kent, the former Katherine Worsley, retired from public life some years ago through ill health, although she occasionally still appears with the rest of the family. She did attend the wedding ceremony of the Duke and Duchess of Cambridge, but she prefers to live away from St James's Palace, in a small flat in central London, or at the family estate, Nettlebed in Oxfordshire, which the Duke visits only when the Duchess is absent. In the days when she was a full-time member of the Royal Family, she would occasionally invite the wives of Members of the Royal Household, who were neighbours in Grace and Favour apartments, to join her for meals when their husbands were abroad with The Queen. However, since her illness, her behaviour is slightly unpredictable, with her servants being invited to call her Kate one day and the next reprimanded for not using her full title. She and her husband now have separate establishments with his office in Kensington Palace and hers on Palace Green.

The Duke's sister, the widowed Princess Alexandra, a first cousin of The Queen, is another person well liked by members of the Household. She plays a full part in the Royal Family 'Firm' for which she receives £225,000 a year. None of this is her salary; every penny goes towards paying her staff and other expenses. The Princess lives alone in a flat in Engine Court, part of St James's Palace, which she shared with her late husband, Sir Angus Ogilvy, and she can often be seen walking alone towards the shops in nearby Jermyn Street. The Princess also has the lease of Thatched House Lodge in Richmond Park in Surrey, acquired by her late husband with a mortgage of £200,000, and she rents a three-bedroom house in Windsor Great

Park for her daughter Marina Mowatt for which she pays a little over £200 a week, which is said to be the market rate.

When the Duke and Duchess of Cambridge were looking for a London base, Princess Alexandra's home was thought to be ideal. It was located inside St James's Palace, so easy to secure and the size would have suited the couple perfectly. However, Princess Alexandra resisted attempts to make her move and her brother Eddie, the Duke of Kent, fought her cause on her behalf. So it was decided to allow her to remain. Apparently, she did not want to move to Kensington Palace, which is where it was intended to rehouse her, on the grounds that she didn't like the idea of 'living in the suburbs'. In other words, too far away from St James's and all the shopping attractions.

So William and Catherine moved to Nottingham Cottage in Kensington Palace, but it is only a temporary address for them. A much more suitable home, nearer Buckingham Palace, will be found within a year or two. It may be called a mere cottage, but it is in fact, a very roomy four-bedroom house, with three bathrooms, an elegant drawing room, dining room, study, and staff quarters. The Queen has approved the spending of £500,000 on bringing the house up to date and installing a modern kitchen for the couple. Local estate agents say if the property came on the market, it would sell for around £3 million or rent for £10,000 a week because of its location and royal provenance. Nottingham Cottage has been lived in in recent years by a succession of senior members of the Royal Household.

York House in St James's Palace contains a number of apartments used as London homes by the Royal Family. The Princess Royal gave up her rooms at Buckingham Palace when she was offered a spacious flat in York House and Princess Beatrice, elder daughter of the Duke of York, must surely have been the envy of all her fellow students at Goldsmith's College, (she graduated in September 2011) with her palatial pad in St James's. Her rooms must be the most exclusive – and expensive – of any of her pals. It is believed that before she moved in, The Queen approved the spending of a quarter of a million pounds in refurbishing the flat that has been described by members of the Household as 'sumptuous'.

Of all the Royals, past and present, one stands out as the most indolent. Prince Henry, Duke of Gloucester, third son of King George V, was a man of whom it was said that if he could have got someone else to breathe for him, he would.

The description is perhaps a little unfair as, along with his brothers, he was totally inhibited by their father and any signs of individuality were quickly stamped out. Also, in his early life he was a modest and easy-going career soldier, but after suffering severe injuries in a car crash, his faculties were impaired and he retired to his home within St James's Palace where his later reputation was earned. Perhaps the kindest way to describe the Duke of Gloucester was to say he was 'uncommunicative'. Shortly before he died in 1974, he was dozing before the fire in his sitting room. This was in the days when they still enjoyed open, coal fires. A footman entered the room and noticed a piece of coal had jumped out of the fire and was burning a hole in the carpet. The man ran across the room and using tongs, picked up the coal and put it back on the fire. Whereupon, the Duke shouted at him, 'Where the bloody Hell have you been. That's been burning like that for ten minutes.' The thought of using the tongs himself simply would not have occurred to him. It was because of such incidents that Prince Henry's reputation grew among the staff. He also liked to 'go commando' when wearing a kilt at Balmoral. And, as he usually sat with his legs wide apart, it was left to his wife to gently remind him to sit in a more gentlemanly fashion.

He was destined for the Regular Army, naturally as an officer, and surprised his parents by doing rather well in his entrance examinations for Sandhurst Military Academy.

When he married, in 1935, Lady Alice Montague-Douglas-Scott, a daughter of the fabulously wealthy Duke of Buccleuch, whose family owned the last private house in Whitehall, it was said that His Grace was not all that pleased and thought it was Prince Henry who was marrying above his station. As it turned out, theirs was a long and successful marriage, and they were the only members of their generation of royalty to actually share a bed, because the Duke hated to sleep alone. Their three sons, one of whom, Prince William, a successful rally driver, was tragically killed in a flying accident in 1972, were, and are, credits to the family. The present Duke of Gloucester, who lives in an elegant thirty-five-roomed apartment in Kensington Palace, carries out a programme of public engagements and his staff have no cause to complain about any lack of good manners, or energy. As long as they maintain a continuous supply of chocolate, he is happy, as he is a self-admitted chocoholic, loving it in every form, liquid or solid.

But the present Duchess of Gloucester is not the favourite member of the family in the opinion of some of the domestic staff. The turnover in the Gloucester Household is faster than in any other Royal Household, and none of it is as a result of the behaviour or attitude of the Duke.

One of the difficulties that servants have to come to terms with is that the Royal Family, with the exception of The Queen, are not always consistent in their dealings with their staff. One day they can appear to be informal and friendly, the next, or even later that same day, something will upset them and the curtain will fall once again. And the servants claim that the Royals they get on with least of all are those who are members of the Royal Family through marriage; in other words, commoners like themselves.

The most successful servants are those who maintain a formal approach to their jobs and never confuse apparent friendliness from the boss with true friendship. Though there are exceptions. Nannies are unique in royal service. They spend more time with their charges than their parents do and frequently are regarded more as surrogate mothers than servants.

The famous, some would say notorious, Bobo McDonald, The Queen's nanny since she was a baby, wielded an influence over the infant Princess Elizabeth that lasted until the day Bobo died, even though she had long retired and the child had been Queen for many years.

Miss McDonald (her sister Ruby was nanny to Princess Margaret) ruled the nursery with a rod of iron and was waited upon by a team of maids throughout her adult life. They were both feared and hated in equal measure by the rest of the Household and together with their cronies, it was said they could have formed a coven.

She served The Queen for sixty years, during which time she was not required to eat with the other staff in the Servants Hall, but had her meals served to her in her own dining room, which, like her sitting room, was decorated and furnished to her own personal taste. Footmen and maids were instructed that they were not to address her personally or meet her eyes if they passed in one of the corridors, and even the Lord Chamberlain knew that when she called him Sir, she didn't really mean it, believing she was superior to everyone else in the Household. And The Queen indulged her every wish. Bobo was also a fearful snob. On one occasion when the then Princess Elizabeth and Prince Philip were staying on the estate of Lord and Lady Brabourne (later Countess Mountbatten of Burma) they were given the use of the cottage in the grounds to afford them a little privacy. When Bobo saw it, she was appalled, calling it a hovel and not fit for 'her Princess'. Later she relented, saying, 'Why can't we have a lovely little cottage just like this one.'

She was also the only person outside the Royal Family who was allowed to call The Queen by her childhood nickname, Lillibet. If any other member of the Household had dared to do so, he or she would have found the Palace doors slammed on them with chilling finality.

In the latter years of her life, Bobo was given the use of a suite of rooms immediately above The Queen's private apartments where Her Majesty would visit her old nanny every day without fail to bring her the latest Palace gossip.

Similarly, Prince Charles's two nannies, Helen Lightbody and Mabel Anderson, became so close to him that it bordered on obsession, on all sides. He came to rely on them so much that when the time came for him to go away to school, it broke his heart, and he sobbed uncontrollably in their arms. It wasn't because he was leaving his mother, but his beloved nannies.

Princess Anne, as ever the no-nonsense sibling, never enjoyed the same relationship with the two nannies. To her they were simply her mother's servants and should be, and were, treated as such. The Household is now holding its breath to see how the new Duke and Duchess of Cambridge, the latest royal couple to set up home, will be thought of by their servants. If early indications are anything to go by, theirs will be a less formal Household than that of any of their family, but with William's future role coming closer every year, it may become necessary for them to adopt a more traditional attitude.

It will be interesting to see where William and Kate come in the servants' royal popularity stakes ten years from now.

N.B. Of the above-mentioned annuities paid to members of the Royal Family, only the £359,000 paid to the Duke of Edinburgh comes out of public funds. The Queen refunds the remainder, some £1,254,000, to the Treasury.

CHAPTER FOUR

THE ROYAL HOUSEHOLD

The Royal Household, and this means those who work at all the royal residences – Buckingham Palace, Windsor Castle, Sandringham, the Palace of Holyroodhouse and Balmoral – employs around 1,200 men and women in a huge variety of posts.

Where else would you find a Liveried Helper, Royal Mews, a Deputy Yeoman of the Royal Cellars, an Education Co-ordinator, a Head of Photographic Services, a Warden at Windsor Castle, a Limner in Ordinary (whatever that is), a Head Coffee Room Maid, Wash-up Assistants, Flower Arranger and Gilders, Cabinet Makers, Locksmiths, a Fender Mender and French Polishers all under the same roof?

They come under the titular head of the Household, the Lord Chamberlain, who in theory is responsible for everything and everybody with the exception of royal funerals and the Coronation. Those are organised by the Earl Marshall, the Duke of Norfolk.

One task that present Lord Chamberlains do not have to contend with any more – but which most of them thoroughly enjoyed at the time – is that of being the 'nation's conscience' – as they were described under The Theatres Act 1843, which gave the Lord Chamberlain responsibility for licensing theatres and making sure nothing 'unsuitable' was performed.

During the twentieth century, the theatre that gave the Lord Chamberlain the most headaches was The Windmill in London, where the first entirely nude revues were staged.

Among the many complaints received was one that stated, 'The two girls with the large balloons were also insufficiently covered about the breasts...' To which the theatre manager, the legendary Vivian Van Damm replied, '...It appears that in the hot weather the elastic holding the tops, which is not of as good quality as normally, is inclined to become slack after a day or so. I have therefore given instructions for this to be renewed whenever necessary.'

It is difficult today to understand what all the fuss was about when anything goes on stage or film. Producers could not show anything depicting royalty until 1937, and the idea of a man and woman together in bed under the same sheet was strictly off-limits. But the Lord Chamberlain and his staff took their responsibilities very seriously, and made frequent visits to the Windmill, and any other theatre where there were doubts about offending public decency. All in the name of duty, of course. No one will admit whether they were reluctant to give up this 'perk' once the Theatres Act 1968 relieved them of such onerous duty. When the Lord Chamberlain or his representative visited the Windmill, or any other theatre where glimpses of the female anatomy might be thought to be offensive, the clerks in the office would often run a book to see what the 'Nipple Count' would be that day. It was a harmless sideline to an otherwise boring daily routine, and the prize money rarely ran to more than a pound or two.

Day in, day out, the business of a modern constitutional monarchy is conducted by a variety of talents ranging from accountants, who balance the royal chequebook, private secretaries, who arrange The Queen's diary, the press office, to make sure the media do not get hold of anything of which they might disapprove, and the Lord Chamberlain's Office, responsible for all ceremonial matters. It was this office that made the arrangements for the wedding of Prince William and Catherine Middleton, now the Duke and Duchess of Cambridge. The Crown Equerry in the Royal Mews and garage controls the transport of any member of the Royal Family by road, whether it's in one of the priceless ornate carriages on a State occasion, or providing a limousine for The Queen and the Duke of Edinburgh anywhere in the country, or just a saloon car to be driven around London.

The Palace kitchens provide up to 600 meals every day, mainly for the 339 full-time staff, and even more when the 215 part-time and honorary positions that obviously do not come in on a daily basis, arrive for a special occasion.

The Household is still a world where liveried servants wait on other servants, where everything stops for Afternoon Tea, though, by tradition, no one sits down in the Equerries Withdrawing Room as they sip their Earl Grey from bone china cups and nibble on cucumber sandwiches. It must surely be the only place left in the world which boasts a Coffee Room Maid, or where a supply of black-edged writing paper and envelopes is kept in case there is a death in the family and the Court goes into mourning. Or which employs a young man one of whose duties is to replace a sheet of black blotting paper on The Queen's desk every morning before she sits down, so that no one could possibly read her writing by holding the pad up to a mirror. He then has the responsibility of destroying the blotting paper, just to make sure.

Although, as stated, the Royal Household employs over a thousand men and women, less than a dozen come into regular contact with The Queen. The majority either wait on other people in the Household, or work in one of the various departments as office staff, accountants, tradesmen, chauffeurs, gardeners and cooks.

The main divisions at Buckingham Palace have remained the same since Queen Victoria's time: Below Stairs, Above Stairs and Out of Doors, though it would be politically incorrect to use those anachronistic terms today. The jobs may be the same, but the titles change with the years.

Instead of scullery maids, they now have kitchen operatives, and housemaids have replaced skivvies. Footmen have remained as they were – with one notable exception, the Palace now employs female footmen after 200 years of restricting the post to men. Equal opportunities have finally caught up with the Royal Household, or perhaps it is the other way around.

Many of the changes to the Household have been definite improvements. Prince Philip earned the undying gratitude of generations of footmen when he dispensed with the ancient custom of them having to powder their hair with an obnoxious substance that took hours to remove. He also did away with the ridiculous system of the two kitchens in the Palace: one for royalty, the other for everyone else. But when he attempted to sell off a number of a range of beautiful copper jelly moulds, he was beaten when he was informed that before they could be sold, all the royal ciphers – some dating back to Queen Victoria's reign – would first of all have to be removed, so he gave up the idea.

But not all the changes have been painless. The streamlining of the staff has meant that men and women who have served for years have been put out to grass, as there simply was not a job for them to do any more. They hated it of course, most of them having known nothing but Palace life since they were old enough to work. But savings had to be made and the Keeper of the Privy Purse and Master of the Household, propelled by the Duke of Edinburgh, wielded the knife with ruthless determination.

There are separate divisions within the Above Stairs category, with Members right at the top, followed by Senior Officials and Officials.

The Members are the people right at the top. Headed by the Lord Chamberlain, Head of the Royal Household, the others all lead the six departments that run the Palace.

The Private Secretary, the Keeper of the Privy Purse, the Master of the Household, the Comptroller of the Lord Chamberlain's Office (the Lord Chamberlain himself has little to do with the everyday running of the department that bears his name), the Crown Equerry and the Director of the Royal Collection.

Immediately beneath these people are the Senior Officials, the men and women such as the Chief Accountants and managers in each department. The day-to-day administration is left in the capable hands of the Officials: the clerks, junior managers and assistant personnel staff. In other words the lower ranks of white-collar workers.

Right at the bottom of the ladder are the Staff: cooks, cleaners, footmen, housemaids, chauffeurs, mechanics and gardeners. And there are also some fifty extra workers based permanently at Buckingham Palace to care for the fabric of the building. These are not on the strength of the Household but employed by the Department of the Environment. The Post Office is run by Royal Mail and while those who work there are also not paid by The Queen, they are allowed to use many of the facilities enjoyed by the regular Palace staff.

One way of telling in which category of royal servant a person falls (and they are all regarded as servants, even the Lord Chamberlain) is to note how they are addressed.

At the very top, Members all call each other by their Christian names, no matter how junior or senior they may be. With one exception. The Lord Chamberlain is always referred to by his title – by everyone. Otherwise, a junior assistant press secretary, who might have joined the Royal Household in recent months, would still be expected to address Sir Christopher Geidt, The Queen's Private Secretary and the most influential man in the Palace, as Christopher. Such informality is taken for granted and doesn't seem to diminish in any way the mutual respect the Members have for each other.

Surnames are always used when referring to Officials. They only use Christian names between men and women of equal rank and status. And it is usually Mr, Mrs or Miss though a few 'Ms's have crept in in recent years when a number of feminists have insisted on being addressed as such.

Staff do not have the problem of trying to distinguish between Members, Senior Officials and Officials. They call everyone Sir or Madam. Though one or two of the longest-serving domestic staff have their own way of saying Sir that lets the recipient know what they really feel.

Angela Kelly, The Queen's senior dresser and now Personal Assistant and Curator of Her Majesty's Jewels, is the servant closest to The Queen in every way. She sees her every day, is a confidante and adviser on the royal wardrobe and although technically she is Staff, and is invariably correct in her dealings with those above her in the Palace hierarchy, they all know she has the ear of The Queen, and are therefore wary when approaching her. She is not a woman anyone, including the Lord Chamberlain, would wish to offend. Not that she parades her superiority. She is a vivacious, outgoing personality who enjoys life to the full, with a splendid apartment near The Queen's quarters at Buckingham Palace and another elegant home in Windsor Great Park. So it is obvious that Her Majesty recognises her worth.

One section of the Household defies being put in a particular category. The ladies-in-waiting to The Queen are unpaid but receive expenses; they are not employed as such but are all personally invited by The Queen, even though she does not make the approach herself. The Mistress of the Robes, always a Duchess, is the senior lady-in-waiting and when there is a vacancy, The Queen will let the Duchess know the name of someone she feels might be suitable. They are all personal friends from the upper classes. This is not because of snobbery, but simply because ladies with this sort of background are more likely to 'know the form' which can be important in royal circles. The Duchess then mentions it to the lady in question in such a way that if she does not wish to join the ranks of the ladies-in-waiting, she can decline without offending Her Majesty. To date, no one has ever refused the honour. When they first meet The Queen in the morning, they give a little curtsy and address her as Your Majesty. Thereafter it is Ma'am. In previous centuries, ladies-in-waiting were political appointments that were highly sought after as they could act as conduits between the Sovereign and Government and even exert some ministerial influence on the monarch (can you imagine Cherie Blair as one of Her Majesty's Women of the Bedchamber?). That power has long since disappeared and the benefits felt by the holders of these posts today is purely of social significance. Even within the ranks of the Ladies-in-Waiting, there are divisions: as stated, right at the top is the Mistress of the Robes, who only appears on special ceremonial occasions such as the State Opening of Parliament when her duties include assisting The Queen to dress in her formal robes at the House of Lords. Next in seniority are the 'Ladies of the Bedchamber' who are all titled, but who have nothing to do with putting Her Majesty to bed. The third category is the Women of the Bedchamber. These are the everyday workhorses and they do not have to be titled, though several of them are. They are on duty two weeks at a time when they have the use of the ladies-in-waiting drawing room where they answer any personal letters The Queen wants written; especially if they are to young children or the very elderly and a note from the private secretary is considered to be too formal.

The Women of the Bedchamber are sometimes referred to within the Household as 'Handbag-holders-in-chief' because they ensure that The Queen has any of the essentials any other woman might require during the engagements on which they accompany her.

When The Queen is planning a visit, either in the United Kingdom or abroad, a small team of three – private secretary, or his representative, protection officer and Lady-in-Waiting – carry out a reconnaissance visit some months in advance. This 'recce' is to go over the proposed programme stopwatch in hand, timing each segment and finding out what is suitable to be presented to Her Majesty.

If a meal is planned, the Lady-in-Waiting agrees the menu with the hosts, stipulating that shellfish must not be served, in case of stomach upsets, and no heavy red meat. Every one of the Ladies has a list of answers to the questions they know they will be asked, with the number one, and most delicate being 'What do we do if Her Majesty wants to go to the loo?' This is the one they always get asked and the answer is always the same. A 'retiring' room should be set aside for the exclusive use of The Queen and the Lady-in-Waiting will indicate if and when it is required.

On one occasion, Her Majesty was due to visit a rugby international to be played at Headquarters, Twickenham, and the then secretary of the Rugby Football Union was the host. When the inevitable query arose, he showed the Lady-in-Waiting the proposed retiring room just off the main grandstand. It was then decided to have a rehearsal or 'dry run' to see if everything worked. Unfortunately, the noise of the cistern could be heard clearly from the nearest seats and the officials were anxious not to cause any embarrassment. So engineers were summoned and the offending water was drained and replaced with straw, which proved to be silent. As it happened, the retiring room was not required after all, but an enterprising England player decided to ensure his place in sporting history by christening the loo himself, long after everyone else had left. His name has never been revealed.

The Royal Family has its own attitude to addressing staff. Police officers (of whatever rank), Pages (with the exception of Her Majesty's personal Page) chauffeurs and older servants are called by their surname. Footmen and valets are known by their Christian name. One young footman, who mistakenly thought this was an invitation to friendliness, replied to one of The Queen's children using his Christian name. By the time the Royal had recovered from the shock, the footman had been removed from royal service and was never heard of again.

Thirty-two porters and non-domestic cleaners are employed at Buckingham Palace, whose duties include moving furniture – and items from the Royal Collection that are valuable but too heavy for one of the footmen or maids to handle. They also help prepare the State Apartments for official functions. It was a team of these porters who manhandled the sections of the giant dining table into the State Ballroom for the dinner party that the Prince of Wales gave on the evening of the wedding of the Duke and Duchess of Cambridge. And they then had to dismantle it the following morning.

Once a year the porters assemble furniture and works of art in Frogmore House, in the grounds of Windsor Castle. The house is no longer used as a royal residence, but the Duke of Edinburgh gives informal dinner parties in its delightful surroundings when the house takes on the splendour of its past history. Frogmore has been open to the public for a specified number of days each year since 1990, so the property has to be maintained in an excellent state of repair.

There is still one department within the Royal Household that is a throwback to previous reigns. It is part of the Lord Chamberlain's Office and is run by someone with the title of State Invitations Assistant. Based in an office in St James's Palace, a small team of nine ladies who go by the quaint description of 'Temporary Lady Clerks' are responsible for writing in longhand over 40,000 invitations a year. These 'Temps', some of whom have been doing the job for over twenty-five years, are the most discreet of women and very few people even know of their existence. Throughout the year they sit and write out the invitations to the four Garden Parties – they are actually called Afternoon Parties – The Queen gives every year: three at Buckingham Palace and one at the Palace of Holyrood House in Edinburgh. The ladies all use fountain pens; they wouldn't dream of using a ballpoint and the invitations are always addressed to the lady of the house, never the husband. This is because the Garden Parties have replaced the old-style Coming Out Balls at which their mothers presented highborn debutantes to the Sovereign. These days, husbands, or partners may accompany their spouse and also a daughter aged eighteen is welcome, but not a son. This is not an occasion for sons, but primarily for daughters.

The staff (they hate that word) in the Garden Party Office could quite easily make considerable sums of money if they were corruptible, as many women (and their husbands) would gladly pay whatever it cost to obtain an invitation to Buckingham Palace. But the assistant and his team have never been tempted. And if anyone even offered a bribe, his or her name would immediately appear on the 'Black List' and they would never be invited. The 'Black List' is a sinister-sounding record of those who have applied to be invited (that's a definite no-no and a guaranteed way to ensure you never are invited) and also it contains letters, some anonymous, suggesting that so-and-so is not the person he or she claims to be and that their title is bogus or their decorations are false. Some of the letters are malicious in the extreme and obviously prompted by jealousy. But every one has to be investigated. The State Invitations Assistant and the 'Temps' are models of propriety at all times. And for this the 'Temps' earn less than £20,000 a year, nearly £5,000 below what is said to be the average income in the United Kingdom.

Because the Royal Household is now so large, it spreads to other buildings such as St James's Palace where the Royal Collection has its headquarters. This is also where the Chancery is located; these are the people who organise the Investitures and make sure every decoration is properly awarded. The Yeomen of the Guard are also housed in St James's Palace, with their ancient titles of Yeoman Bed Goer and Yeoman Bed Hanger. Their Captain is a political appointment, usually a Deputy Chief Whip in the House of Lords, who, no doubt, is relieved that he will not suffer the fate of one of his illustrious predecessors, Sir Walter Raleigh, who was taken to the Tower of London and executed.

The Royal Archives and Library are situated inside Windsor Castle and this is also the home to the Military Knights of Windsor, former officers who live in attractive houses alongside King Henry VIII's Gate, the main entrance to the castle. The Knights attend morning service in St George's Chapel and they are always on duty at the annual Garter Ceremony. One bone of contention among former officers, of a certain gender, is that there are no female Military Knights, and according to the present contingent, there never will be.

The whole business of sex discrimination and race in the Royal Household has been raised many times. Even Prince Charles has been heard to claim there are far too few black employees or anyone from ethnic minorities.

No one would claim the Royal Household is perfect and even The Queen has been criticised for not appointing a personal attendant from an ethnic minority. Of course, she does have two permanent Ghurkha officers at Court, but non-white faces are few and far between.

Those who run the organisation say the reason is that very few ethnic minority men and women apply. If they did, they would be considered in exactly the same way as white applicants. There wouldn't be any positive discrimination which would be just as patronising.

As far as The Queen is concerned it wouldn't matter if a person were black, white, brown or yellow. If he or she were the right person for the job they would get it. Her Majesty is arguably the least prejudiced person in the United Kingdom and throughout her sixty years on the Throne she has entertained in her homes men and women of every race, colour and creed.

But if there is one stipulation that The Queen makes it is that she prefers dealing with men than women. Which is why no woman has ever been appointed Lord (or Lady) Chamberlain, or to the most important role in the Household, that of Private Secretary. A Crown Equerry riding sidesaddle is also an unlikely sight in the near future, but if a female financial whiz kid emerged as a possible future Keeper of the Privy Purse, Her Majesty would raise no objections. Where royalty is concerned, money has no gender.

But, as the former Archbishop of Canterbury, the late Robert Runcie, said, 'As far as The Queen is concerned we are all the same. It doesn't matter if you are the man who stokes the boilers or the Lord Chamberlain. She treats everyone in exactly the same way. We are all servants. She may become attached to one or two (Bobo McDonald, her former Nanny, is a perfect example) but everyone is a servant and nothing more, and when you fall off the twig, that's it. It is as if you were never there in the first place.' It's 'them' and 'us' at its most basic.

While The Queen appreciates the hard work and dedication of her staff, she has been there longer than any of them, and she does not place too much reliance on any of them, no matter how important they may think they are to her. She knows that the moment one departs, for whatever reason, a replacement will be found immediately. It's the only way she can live her life. Twenty years is a long time for a royal servant to remain at the Palace. The Queen has been on the Throne three times that long already. Prime Ministers, Popes and Presidents have come and gone during her reign and there is no servant working in the Royal Household today who was there when The Queen moved in to Buckingham Palace in 1952.

The Royal Household continues to be a place of privilege and protocol, snobbery and prestige, and not all of it above stairs either.

There is still the same amount of jockeying for position as they all realise that proximity to the Monarch is where the power lies.

In the early days of The Queen's reign any young man or woman who was taken on as a junior footman or housemaid by the Master of the Household considered they were the luckiest people in the land – and they were expected to show that gratitude on a daily basis. Metaphorical forelock tugging was a daily requirement.

Today, new recruits are more confident, better educated, healthier and, as a result, more independent. The days of extreme reverence and deference are over. In the past, no junior employee would dream of answering back to a superior on pain of instant dismissal. Today, if a footman believes he is in the right, he will stand his ground – knowing he has the backing of his union helps – but it still might not do his promotion chances any good.

This Household, and by that I include those of The Queen's children, was once an organisation where nepotism ruled supreme. Jobs were handed down from father to son, generation to generation. Today, it is not quite like that. These days, it has become more – but not fully – a meritocracy.

Promotion is slow; the money is poor, while the living conditions have barely changed in 100 years. Yet there is still a never-ending line; an unending supply, of candidates willing to devote some, but no longer all, of their working lives in the service of the most famous family in the world.

The Queen takes an extraordinary interest in every aspect of her Household, from the most junior domestic servants to the family life of some of her most senior aides even if it is in a strictly 'hands off' manner.

Her former Lord Chamberlain, the late Lord (Chips) Maclean was once asked how involved Her Majesty was with the Household. He replied, without hesitation, 'Why, she runs the place.'

CHAPTER FIVE

WHY WORK FOR ROYALTY?

The Royal Household actively encourages recruitment in practically all its categories, offering a wide range of benefits and rewards. What they don't offer is high salaries. Nobody joins the Household just for the money – or if they do, they are soon disappointed. Most of the jobs available at Buckingham Palace are better paid outside, but none compares in terms of prestige. And young men and women soon realise that a couple of years' service with fairly rigid discipline and poor wages can practically guarantee an open door to more lucrative employment elsewhere. Nothing influences would-be employers – particularly foreigners – more than a reference written on paper headed with the royal crest.

One former footman at Buckingham Palace left after three years and was immediately snapped up by an American billionaire who not only paid him

$75,000 a year to be his butler, but provided him with a house and two cars: one for himself and another for his wife.

If a young man or woman is starting out on a career in catering or hotel management, he or she cannot do better than a few years working for The Queen.

It is still possible to obtain employment simply by turning up at the side door of Buckingham Palace (it's the one alongside The Queen's Gallery) and asking for a job. You won't be turned away. Everyone is seen. But the days when that was all it took are long gone and with security now of prime importance, every applicant – and they receive over 4,000 every year – is vetted and thoroughly checked after they have completed the complicated application form, that takes at least an hour to fill in.

And in this age of technology, when every young man and woman is computer literate, the Palace advertises on the internet, so attracts interest from all over the world. They also stress that diversity is the name of the game, so people of every race, religion and sexual orientation are encouraged to apply. But, so far, the number of black front of house staff at Buckingham Palace can be counted on the fingers of both hands.

Technical colleges in Britain are breeding grounds for junior Palace staff and the students cut their teeth by being sent to help out at State Banquets as assistant waiters to give them an idea of what could lay ahead if they decided to apply.

Buckingham Palace has twelve footmen and just three footwomen (who are still called footmen) and they will not increase this ratio. The reason is that footmen have to be able to be used as valets from time to time when male visitors are expected and female valets would not be suitable as they could find themselves in a compromising situation.

An applicant for a job as footman is seen by the Sergeant Footman, the 'foreman' of this section of the Master of the Household's department. If he passes this test he is then interviewed by the Deputy Master and asked lots of questions about his family background, how much he knows about the Royal Family, why does he want to work here, is he prepared to travel, does he like flying – they used to ask if he suffered from sea-sickness, but since 1997, when the Royal Yacht *Britannia* was decommissioned, that no longer applies – does he have a girlfriend and are there any plans for marriage. The Queen prefers single men as domestic staff, and the Deputy Master also tests his social skills. If he successfully passes this interview he is offered a short-term contract, usually six weeks, to see 'if we like each other'. What this really means is, if the Palace approves.

Then the new boy, or girl, is taken to the Livery Room on the first floor to be fitted out with his uniforms, including the State Livery, some of which dates back to previous reigns. So it doesn't do to be too choosey or to think too carefully about who and how many people have worn the kit before you. The reason for using old livery is that a new set would cost well over £2,000 and as some of the footmen do not stay all that long it wouldn't make economic sense to provide every one with a new set. The gilt jackets are also very heavy to wear, 28lbs (12.7kg) so the footmen need to be fairly fit and strong, as they will be wearing them for several hours at a State Banquet.

Footmen are given a set of 'guidelines', which includes no beard as Her Majesty does not care for facial hair. She's not too keen on moustaches either. They are also warned not to wear perfume or after-shave that is too pungent and hair should be kept fairly short. Jewellery is restricted to a watch, and definitely no pierced ears or other parts of the face sporting decoration. Tattoos are also frowned upon, but if they are hidden beneath one's clothes, no one objects.

There is a preferred minimum height requirement of 5ft 8ins and as a footman standing at 6ft 6ins would obviously stick out like a sore thumb at a State Banquet, nobody of this height would be employed unless he was thought to be of exceptional quality, though there is no hard and fast rule on the upper levels.

Similarly, most front of house staff are of slim build – partly to fit the existing uniforms and partly for the symmetry. At Buckingham Palace nothing is allowed to mar the pristine appearance of everything and everyone. At a banquet even the potatoes and sprouts are measured before they are served to make sure they are of similar dimensions so they won't spoil the appearance of the dinner plate.

New recruits are required to live in and are allocated a room on the top floor right at the rear of the Palace. For obvious reasons it's called the Footmen's Floor. The rooms are small and cramped and not popular because the walls between them are wafer thin so there is not much privacy. Each one is furnished with a single bed – married men live out in one of the Grace and Favour houses or apartments – a chest of drawers, a wardrobe to hang livery and uniforms, a table, one easy chair and a washbasin, with constant hot water. There are no private bathrooms on this floor.

When the footman moves up the ladder to become a page or valet he moves to the Pages' Floor at the front of the Palace, with one of the best views in London, straight down The Mall, overlooking the Victoria Memorial, or The Wedding Cake as the staff irreverently refer to it.

Here the rooms are much larger and brighter, with a kitchenette and shared bathroom between two occupants.

The chefs are regarded as professionals, a cut above the footmen, so they are given bed-sitting rooms on the 'Pages' Floor. But even here there are rivalries. If a larger or better room becomes vacant there is an almighty rush to get it, so if it is heard that one of the Pages is leaving or moving on, the others all start to lobby the Deputy Master of the Household, trying to get a head start.

In the early days of The Queen's reign, servants were expected to be seen and not heard. Their social life was unimportant and for most employees of the Sovereign it was a case of work to bed and bed to work with little time off for outside activities.

Today, all that is a thing of the past. The Royal Household tries to keep its staff as long as possible by making working and living conditions attractive and inviting.

Recruits can join seven different sports and social clubs, with Football, Cricket, Golf, Bowls, Tennis,

Squash and a Swimming Pool available. There is a licensed bar at Buckingham Palace and at Windsor Castle where drinks are subsidised, while the Sport and Social Club secretary organises Bonfire Night parties, theatre trips and, of course, bingo.

Servants are allowed to invite visitors to their rooms, with the Master of the Household's prior permission, with the caveat that they should leave by midnight. But some of the younger men and women smuggle partners in for the night and no one seems to mind – or even to know. Though it must be a bit of a tight squeeze with the single bed situation in the servants' quarters.

As most of the footmen and housemaids are young men and women, there is a certain amount of social intercourse. It usually takes place at what they call 'Corridor Parties' in the long alleys between their rooms. Anyone who happens to be staying in hears about the party, music is provided by one of them bringing a collection of CDs (as long as there is not too much noise) and everyone brings a bottle. It's all harmless fun – and it's cheap, and no one has to drive home afterwards. This is also where many of the pranks are played on newcomers. One junior footman, who unusually happened to be over six feet tall, arrived on his first night to find that the sheets on his bed had been folded back to half their normal size. In other words he had been given an 'apple-pie' bed. Thinking this was the way the Royal Household preferred it to be, the poor man slept for a week with his knees tucked up under his chin, before they took pity on him and revealed it was a joke. He told me he thought it was because the Master of the Household was trying to save money by using only half the sheets.

The protocol that controls life above stairs in all the royal residences, with those higher up the Line of Succession taking precedence over those lower down, even among siblings, is repeated below stairs.

The Palace Steward, the most senior member of The Queen's domestic Household, would not dream of having a quiet drink with a junior footman and if he saw the Page of the Chambers, his deputy, socialising with someone below him in the Palace hierarchy, he would have a word, warning him to 'maintain his dignity' and 'remember your position'. Both these men began their careers as junior footmen, so they know the score, having learned their place many years earlier.

When the Court moves, say from Buckingham Palace to Balmoral, the servants who are accompanying The Queen travel in order of seniority. If they are flying, the royal chef knows he will be allocated a better seat than one of his kitchen staff. If he wasn't he would refuse to travel.

The Queen's Page will be seated somewhere near the front of the aircraft, along with one of Her Majesty's dressers. Footmen will be at the rear. The Master of the Household allocates seats in aircraft and trains and says the tantrums can occur even for a short journey by coach from London to Windsor. One older servant sulked for days when he was forced to sit next to a housemaid. He even asked the Sergeant Footman to bring the matter up at the next staff meeting.

But when they are moving house, even the most junior staff benefit from the system that has been refined over the years. Their luggage is collected from outside their rooms and by the time they arrive at Balmoral, or wherever it may be, the bags will be waiting for them.

The ten weeks in the summer The Queen and the Duke of Edinburgh spend at Balmoral is the highlight of the year for the Royal Family, if not exactly for the staff.

It's a busy time for the servants, with guests to provide for and those interminable picnics so beloved of royalty to organise.

The Queen gives two Ghillies Balls in the Castle to which all the estate workers, inside and out, are invited. Traditional Scottish dancing is the order of the day with the royal ladies in Royal Stuart sashes and the gentlemen in kilts.

Detachments from one of the Scottish regiments are based at the Castle during The Queen's holiday and one of their duties is to learn the intricate steps of all the Scottish dances as they too are among the guests.

It's a very democratic evening, with the carpenters and gamekeepers partnering the Princess Royal and the other royal ladies, while Charles, Andrew and Edward take the maids and dressers onto the floor.

An elderly aunt of Prince Philip's once found herself dancing with a very personable young man. As the staff are warned that they should never initiate conversation with royalty, the man stayed silent until the aunt asked what he did, thinking he might be a distant nephew she had never met. When he replied that he worked as a boatman on Loch Muick (where Charles and Anne were taught to sail by their father), she told him that her husband, who was in fact a Grand Duke, had also wanted to be in the navy, so they would have had a lot in common. It's that sort of evening. The next morning everyone was back in his rightful place.

It's perhaps just as well that entertainment at Balmoral is home grown, as there is little else to do for healthy young men and women, which is why they all prefer to be in London or Windsor where the bright lights are near at hand.

Where the Royal Family's entertainment is concerned, their tastes rarely change. Sporting activities in the daytime with the male members apparently enjoying themselves lying in damp gorse for hours at a time stalking a stag. Before the Court moves to Balmoral, the Master of the Household contacts Her Majesty's Page to find out which films and television they would most like to see. These are then obtained from the distributors, BBC, ITV and Channel 4, free of charge and shown either in the private cinema at the Castle or placed in one of the video recorders.

The Queen's senior dresser is contacted to find out which books Her Majesty and His Royal Highness are interested in and copies are placed in the library at Balmoral or in the bedrooms as both The Queen and Prince Philip like to read in bed.

There cannot be many places in London where the staff can claim that they use The Queen's swimming pool. Buckingham Palace's indoor pool is located at the rear of the building, on the right hand side as you look from the front.

The Staff Sports Club allows its members to use the pool at certain specified times, when no member of the Royal Family wants to swim. The rule is if a staff member is swimming and one of the Royals appears, they have to get out, unless invited to remain, which often happens. If when the staff member turns up a Royal is already in the pool, the servant, and this includes senior Members such as the Private Secretary or Keeper of the Privy Purse, will not attempt to join them. It's a rule that seems to work well, and these days the Duke of Edinburgh is the only permanent royal resident at the Palace who still uses the pool regularly. But it is expected that the Duke and Duchess of Cambridge may well avail themselves of the privilege when they take up residence in their London apartment at Kensington Palace.

There is a thriving film society in the Royal Household, which meets once a month to view the latest releases in the Buckingham Palace cinema. It is free to staff and they manage to obtain any film they want long before it is on general release.

Perhaps one of the main benefits is that anyone in the Royal Household is able to get tickets to any theatre or concert hall in London. Managers keep back a supply of seats for the Palace and most of these are complimentary, including at the Royal Albert Hall.

The only place where they have to take their turn is the Royal Opera House at Covent Garden, where the Royal Box is reserved strictly for members of the family. As Prince Charles is the only one who is passionate about opera, he uses the box frequently and even if the others want to see a performance, they have to check with him first to see if he is going. He takes precedence over everyone except The Queen and as she never goes to the opera anyway, the Royal Box is his personal fiefdom.

Tickets to Test matches at Lords and The Oval are always available and among the most highly prized are those reserved for members of the Royal Household at Wimbledon. The family are able to use the Royal Box at the invitation of the President of the All England Club, while middle management officials usually find they are relegated to seats some way back. But they are still worth having, so no one abuses the privilege and tries to sell them on.

The Household football, cricket, bowls and golf clubs have no difficulty in finding fixtures as every club wants to be entertained on a royal sports ground or golf course. And they love having correspondence written on Buckingham Palace headed paper.

New recruits are told what to do if they should meet The Queen during the day. The rule is that they should stand still until she has passed and they should not speak unless she addresses them first, which she often does, even if it is only just a mere nod of the head.

But servants no longer have to hide behind the curtains if they see a member of the Royal Family approaching as they did in the early days of The Queen's reign; not on her orders, but those of the Master of the Household. And neither is a maid instantly dismissed if she hasn't finished her work by noon, as she would have been in the past.

The Queen takes a personal interest in her Household and wants to know everything that's going on below stairs as well as with her senior officials. With her personal staff – Ladies-in-Waiting, Pages, dressers, maids and footmen – she can be very friendly, particularly if she is alone in her sitting room during the evening. She will often engage whoever is on duty in conversation asking about their family, and even if they have any pets. But it's always a one-way conversation. The Queen never discusses her own family with anyone.

At one time there were five dining rooms for staff at Buckingham Palace: the Household Dining Room where the Members were served by uniformed servants and where the menus were all printed in French; the Senior Officials Dining Room, where those in that category also ate their meals in splendid surroundings; the Officials Dining Room, not quite as grand but still rather like an officer's Mess; the Stewards Hall, presided over by the Palace Steward and where his senior domestic colleagues enjoyed being waited on by junior staff; and the Servants Hall, where everyone else had their breakfast, lunch and dinner.

A recent Lord Chamberlain, supported by the Duke of Edinburgh, decided in the interests of economy – and in spite of protests from all concerned – to abolish all these different dining rooms and amalgamate them into a single central establishment that is now known simply as The Dining Room.

It is situated on the first floor, overlooking Buckingham Palace Road, near the side entrance to the Palace, and the entire Household eats there.

On any working day, you might find the Lord Chamberlain and The Queen's Private Secretary queuing up alongside the most junior footman to receive their food on a tray from the Servery. It's a very democratic system, that certainly saves a lot of money, but it's not universally popular. Also the Dining Room no longer serves alcohol, which again does not go down too well.

On the recent State Visit of President Obama of the United States, the Dining Room was overwhelmed by the hundreds of secret service personnel accompanying the President and his wife, who swamped the room at breakfast and refused to stand in line, saying it was not the 'American' way.

There is still a Household Dining Room that is normally not open every day. But when the occasion demands, such as visits from foreign Households, the Members are able to use its facilities. And most of them love the genteel atmosphere redolent of one of the older gentlemen's clubs.

Benefits

The prestige alone of working for the most famous family in the world is no longer sufficient to attract the cream of domestic staff to the Royal Household. They have been forced to make concessions that in previous years were unnecessary.

Once a footman or housemaid has served a six-month probationary period, they are eligible for health cover and to join the Royal Household Stakeholder pension scheme. The Queen pays 15 per cent employer's contribution into the scheme on the servant's behalf and if a staff member should die while in service, there is a death benefit payment amounting to four times the annual salary.

Among the other benefits, all staff are entitled to twenty-five days' annual leave, rising to twenty-seven after three years' service and thirty days after ten years. Part-time staff receive leave on a pro rata basis.

As some of the staff have to travel into central London from their homes, they are granted interest-free loans to buy season tickets, some of which can cost several thousand pounds a year.

Everybody who works at Buckingham Palace is entitled to a free lunch on the days they are working, and staff quite frequently pop in, even when they are off duty, to take advantage of the offer. The Master of the Household knows this happens, but he prefers to turn a blind eye. If it keeps his staff happy, what's the harm?

The Household, and this includes those working for other members of the Royal Family, offers an attractive car-leasing scheme with staff able to rent vehicles at discount rates. Until a few years ago, this included luxury makes such as Jaguar and top-of-the-range Rovers. But the scheme now applies only to middle-of-the-range makes and models. It still accounts for savings up to £2,000 a year in some cases, so it is a benefit well worth having, particularly for those who are based in royal residences miles away from London.

The Household prides itself on being family friendly. So it offers not only maternity and paternity leave but also leave to those who are adopting children or men and women who require fertility treatment.

Among the hidden benefits of working for the Royal Family is the cash-in-hand supply that every servant worth his salt knows about and one or two exploit.

There are plenty of opportunities for a little private enterprise on the side if you know where to look and who to approach, particularly during the summer season when the Palace is open to paying visitors. A small number of staff – and this includes the 'temps' employed just for the summer period – are able to tell which visitors might be amenable to a little 'arrange-ment'. It could be just family or friends who are visit-ing the Palace and are looking for a bargain, so there's no real harm in a staff member using his discount in the shops for their benefit.

A year-round benefit is the 'moonlighting' that goes on. For many years domestic staff have run a tiny but profitable sideline in working for outside parties, serving drinks and canapés, waiting at dinner tables or just opening doors. They do not wear their offi-cial uniform but each one has something that to the untrained eye passes for the next best thing.

There is a 'fixer' in every department of the Palace who will arrange for a couple, or however many are required, to serve at these functions, and the Master of the Household and the Royal Family turn a blind eye. They all know what's going on. Both The Queen and Prince Philip have found themselves being served cocktails by their own staff from time to time, and Prince Philip in particular will often give a wink to a young housemaid, 'moonlighting' as a waitress, just to let her know he is in on the secret.

The Master of the Household actually encourages some of his younger staff to work outside as it gives them additional experience, as well as helping them financially. The going rate is around £10 an hour for a waiter or waitress; £15 an hour for a fully trained butler and £20 an hour for one of the royal chefs.

There are also a couple of footmen who visit houses in nearby Belgravia once a week to polish and shine all the boots and shoes on the premises. The going rate is around £20 a time.

There's only one rule: it's a strictly cash business. No cheques or credit cards accepted.

The regimental bands that play in the Palace forecourt every morning during Changing the Guard, also have their own little sidelines. Anyone with the money can hire any combination from a trio to a full orchestra, to play in their off-duty hours. Their repertoire runs from well-known excerpts from opera and ballet, to the big band sounds of the 1940s and 1950s to rock'n'roll and anything in between. For the bandsmen (and women) it makes a nice change from the military marches they are required to play every morning and they love letting their hair down.

The bandmasters all welcome their musicians accepting these 'gigs' and there's nothing 'under-the-counter' about the arrangement. It is all done with the blessing of the regiment and the Ministry of Defence.

CHAPTER SIX

THE DECISION MAKERS

ess than a dozen people right at the top of the Royal Household earn more than £100,000 a year, with several hundred down at the bottom on less than £20,000. So nobody joins the Household in order to get rich. If they do they are soon disillusioned. The top echelon consists of those who run the Palace – the people whose decisions affect not only the rest of the Household, but The Queen herself.

The most important and influential person at Buckingham Palace is The Queen's principal private secretary, Sir Christopher Geidt, but he is not the highest paid. That honour goes to Sir Alan Reid, Keeper of the Privy Purse, in other words, the man who controls the royal chequebook and who pays everyone else. His salary is £180,000 a year compared with Christopher Geidt's £146,000 (a slight increase on David Cameron's £142,500), but both these salaries are down on what they were paid the previous year.

Number three in the money stakes is Air Vice-Marshal David Walker, Master of the Household, who earns £120,000 a year, up from £112,000 last year. Lt Col. Andrew Ford is Comptroller of the Lord Chamberlain's Office, the man who organises all royal ceremonials, and he is paid £101,000, a comparatively modest increase of £100 a week on his last year's salary of £96,000.

Their titular boss, The Lord Chamberlain, the Rt Hon. The Earl Peel is paid less than any of his department heads with an annual salary of £82,000 (up £1,000) but his is considered to be a part-time appointment and he is expected to be inside the Palace for only a few days each week. However, most of the recent Lord Chamberlains have taken their jobs very seriously, and they work practically full-time.

In addition to these salaries, the men mentioned above all have payments made into their pension plans.

Air Vice-Marshal Walker is on secondment from the Ministry of Defence on a contract that is reviewed every year (he actually retired from the RAF in August 2011 with the rank of Air Marshal) while Lt Col. Andrew Ford is paid in line with Senior Civil Service pay scales, plus a performance-related pay element up to a maximum of 4.5 per cent.

Apart from the two just mentioned the salaries of the others are set by the Royal Household Remuneration Committee whose members at the time of writing are: The Cabinet Secretary, Sir Gus O'Donnell, The Permanent Secretary to the Treasury,

Sir Nicholas Macpherson, the Lord Chamberlain (the only member of the Royal Household allowed responsibility for setting his colleagues' salaries) and the Treasury Officer of Accounts and Secretary to the Committee, Paula Diggle.

The non-executive members of the Committee are not paid for their duties.

While the salaries of these top men might seem generous to outsiders, where the average annual income is said to be £25,000, any of them could leave tomorrow and move into commerce and more than double their salary overnight.

Christopher Geidt is not only The Queen's senior adviser at the Palace; he is also one of the most influential people in the United Kingdom. After the election of 2010 when there was no clear winner, it was Geidt who advised Her Majesty to appoint David Cameron as Prime Minister, only when a decision was 'clear and uncontroversial'. In this way he protected his royal mistress from becoming embroiled in party politics.

He liaises with his opposite number at 10 Downing Street in the Prime Minister's office.

Christopher Geidt is the power behind the Throne; the man The Queen trusts above all others outside the family. He guides her not only through the lines of communication between the Palace and Government, but also between herself and the Presidents and Prime Ministers of all Commonwealth countries.

He is her eyes and ears and since he joined the Royal Household in 2002 as an assistant private secretary – he got the top job in 2007 – he has forced the Household into adopting modern business practices, so that today an air of professionalism is felt throughout Buckingham Palace.

One of the secrets of his success with The Queen is his ability to tell her what she needs to know, rather than what he feels she might want to hear, as some of her early private secretaries were wont to do.

Until the advent of Sir William Heseltine (1986–90) an outgoing Australian, who was a breath of fresh air, private secretaries had been recruited for their diplomatic skills through the 'old boy' network, rather than for any experience of the outside world.

Christopher Geidt is the latest (following Robin Janvrin and Robert Fellowes) who is a realist and pragmatist, and who is not afraid to speak his mind, even if by doing so it might make him unpopular.

One quality he shares with his predecessors is his attention to detail, which is legendary in an organisation where it is taken for granted that everything runs to time.

Christopher Geidt, as a former soldier in intelligence, believes implicitly in forward planning. He anticipates problems before they arise and knows the answers to any questions almost before they are asked.

A Cambridge graduate, he speaks several languages and he was asked by The Queen to help shape Prince William's image before he emerged on the royal scene as the latest generation of the family to undertake public duties.

When one looks at the responsibilities that the private secretary assumes – liaison with the armed forces (he is the only private secretary to The Queen who was not commissioned, but served as a sergeant), the sometimes tricky relationship with the Archbishop of Canterbury and then handling the hundreds of organisations, both civil and military with which Her Majesty is associated – it is not difficult to see how he earns his £2,800 a week. The Queen believes he is worth every penny and he justified her confidence with his organisation of her visit to Ireland in May 2011, which is regarded as one of the most successful of her reign – in what could have been the most difficult circumstances.

The Queen recognised Christopher Geidt's value to her in the 2011 Birthday Honours List when she made him a Knight Commander of the Royal Victorian Order, her personal Order of Chivalry which she awards without advice from or reference to anyone, including the Prime Minister. To be invited to join the Royal Victorian Order is the biggest compliment The Queen can pay one of her staff and the new Sir Christopher, as one of the latest recruits, is fully aware of the honour.

During his military service, Sir Christopher acted as an interrogator in Bosnia, using skills he has since brought to the Royal Household. He knows how to ask the right question to the right person at exactly the right time – and how to evaluate an answer correctly. He's a difficult man to bluff.

As the chief executive of 'House of Windsor Ltd' he is the first man at his desk in the morning and often the last to leave at night. But he is not a one-man-band. A large and efficient team of assistant private secretaries and deputies support him, knowing that no matter how hard they work, he works even harder. He insists that his office is a team effort, but his staff know that in every team there has to be a captain and there is no doubt who it is in this department. In securing Christopher Geidt, The Queen is said to have made the bargain of the year. He could easily walk into a top job in the City and command a salary of at least £500,000 a year.

KEEPER OF THE PRIVY PURSE

Although the Private Secretary is the most important man in the Royal Household, he is not the highest paid. That distinction goes to the Keeper of the Privy Purse, which in modern terms means the man who controls the royal chequebook and everything else to do with spending at the Palace. That is why he is paid £40,000 a year more than the Private Secretary. Royalty always follows the golden rule: Go where the money is.

The Keeper is one of the oldest positions in the Royal Household dating back to the beginning of the eighteenth century. Apart from two early appointments, every Keeper of the Privy Purse has been a man. The exceptions were Sarah Churchill, Duchess of Marlborough, who served Queen Anne from 1702–1711 to be followed by Baroness [Abigail] Masham who continued until George I came to the throne in 1714. Since then the post has been a male-dominated province.

The present Keeper, Sir Alan Reid, has held the top job since 2002, and is only the second person appointed to this prestigious role to be a professional accountant. The first was his immediate predecessor, Sir Michael Peat, both of whom came from the same stable as head of the leading international accountancy firm, KPMG. Prior to this, all the Keepers had traditionally been former military men with little or no expertise in financial matters.

The Keeper looks after The Queen's private financial affairs, including her bank account, which is held at Coutts in The Strand, now part of National Westminster, which in turn is an arm of the Royal Bank of Scotland.

Coutts not only provides The Queen with her chequebook, but every other member of the Royal Family, and they have done so, with the utmost discretion, since 1760, when King George III became the first British monarch to open an account with them – and to take advantage of their overdraft facilities.

However, Coutts, unlike other royal suppliers, do not hold a Royal Warrant. This is because bankers are 'professionals' like doctors and lawyers, and only 'tradesmen' such as shopkeepers, plumbers and butchers, are eligible for the warrants. The Royal Warrants have been in existence since the Middle Ages and are awarded only to tradesmen and suppliers of goods. They are a mark of recognition of excellent service to members of the Royal Family. At the present time only The Queen, the Duke of Edinburgh and the Prince of Wales award warrants and the recipients are allowed to display the Royal Arms on their products as well as the legend 'By Appointment to...' The town with the largest number of Warrant Holders is

Ballater, near Balmoral, where practically every tiny shop and business is able to show it has served royalty for generations.

The Keeper of the Privy Purse has a thankless task in that other departments within the Royal Household do not like many of the decisions he is forced to make on the grounds of economy.

If the Master of the Household wants to spend money on refurbishing staff accommodation or new outfits for his footmen, he has to go cap in hand to the Keeper for approval. It is not always forthcoming, as the Keeper has different priorities. He has to look at the broader picture, always remembering that at the end of the year he has to balance the books.

The accounts are kept in immaculate order. Bills are paid promptly, with discounts negotiated wherever possible. The Keeper has registered Her Majesty for Value Added Tax, as a business, which means she pays 20 per cent on nearly everything she buys, but as long as it is for business reasons, she is then able to claim it all back, and she has the use of the money for three months as VAT is paid every quarter.

Another of the Keeper's responsibilities is to ensure that when members of the Royal Family, or the Household, travel abroad, foreign currency is obtained at the best rates and at zero commission.

Apart from The Queen herself, the Keeper of the Privy Purse is the only person in the world who knows the full extent of her wealth. How much cash she has; how many shares and in what companies and all her other investments. Even the Duke of Edinburgh does not know the intimate details of his wife's fortune.

So it is just as well that he is totally uninterested in finances anyway.

One would think that Coutts, as her bankers, would be aware of Her Majesty's worth. But they only know what the Keeper and his staff allow them to know. As The Queen no longer writes personal cheques, because people had a habit of not cashing them but preferring to keep them as mementoes, which, in turn, caused chaos in the royal accounts, her bank has only a limited knowledge of her wealth. But it is a fair guess to say that she is not overdrawn, and never has been, even if her mother was said to have died with an overdraft at Coutts of over £2 million – which was settled on her death by The Queen.

Within the Keeper of the Privy Purse's department there is a small sub-department known as the Royal Almonry. The Lord High Almoner, the Lord Bishop of Rochester, heads this ancient-sounding office. In centuries past, this office was responsible for distributing alms to the poor on behalf of the Monarch. Today it has but one task, to look after the administrative details of the annual Maundy Service when The Queen gives a bag full of specially minted coins, to the deserving men and women of different parishes in the realm. The bag gets heavier each year, as the number of coins equals one for each year of her life.

Apart from Her Majesty's public funds, the Privy Purse office also controls all payments made from her private sources. The Queen makes considerable gifts to charity every year; some of which are well-known organisations, while others are simply individual cases that have been brought to her attention by her family or members of the Household. There is only one condition attached to these gifts; no publicity is allowed, on Her Majesty's strict instructions. She is already the recipient of hundreds of begging letters every year and if it were revealed that she had responded to any of them, the floodgates would open and she would be deluged.

The Queen's racing interests are widely known and the Treasurer's office liaises with her racing manager regarding the expenses incurred. She has been heard to say that owning a racehorse is like fitting a tap to your pocket. And as wealthy as she undoubtedly is, there is a limit to what she can afford. In the world of racing, Her Majesty is not even in the front rank when it comes to buying the best horses. The oil-rich Middle-East sheiks and one or two Irish owners leave her standing when it comes to bidding wars. And she has yet to achieve her lifelong ambition of owning a winner of The Derby.

The Keeper of the Privy Purse is Receiver-General of the Duchy of Lancaster and he works closely with The Queen's bankers, Coutts, and also with her legal advisers, the old-established firm of Farrers in the city of London. It was Farrers who handed the divorces of Prince Margaret and Lord Snowdon, Princess Anne and Mark Phillips, the Prince and Princess of Wales and the Duke and Duchess of York. For them it was all in a day's work.

Farrer & Co, to give them their proper title, was founded in 1701, since when it has been continuously associated with royalty. In 1788, the then Duke of York borrowed money from Farrer and also from his bankers Coutts and the following year, 1789, Farrers acted for the Duke of York when he successfully sued *The Times* for libel after they suggested he and his brother were not altogether delighted at the recovery of their father, George III. The editor of the paper was sent to prison for a year.

Farrer & Co has had a long list of celebrity clients including, in 1854, Charles Dickens, who employed them when he was buying a property.

Every member of British royalty since the beginning of the eighteenth century has had cause to thank the company for its dedication to their well-being in legal matters. Farrer & Co probably know more royal secrets than anyone else in the world.

The Keeper of the Privy Purse is supported by a large team of professionals, with forty-six men and women in his office and a further seventy-three in the adjoining Finance and Property Branch, where they administer the salaries, pensions and the Personnel Office. They even have a small staff devoted to the supply of stationery throughout the Palace. People sometimes wonder how it is that within hours of a royal death being announced, all letters and envelopes sent from the Royal Household are black-edged. It's simply because this office maintains a permanent supply, ready for any such occasion.

Apart from the Keeper himself and his two senior deputies – the Director of Finance and Director of Property Services, both of whom earn over £90,000 a year – salaries are relatively modest in this department, even though the requirements for positions can be demanding. For instance, at the time of writing a Systems Support Officer is needed, based at Buckingham Palace. The specification for the job includes being educated to degree level, having excellent IT skills, accurate documentation skills and holding a current driving licence in case he or she is needed to work at another royal location. And for all this, the successful applicant will be paid the princely sum of £19,055 a year.

THE MASTER OF THE HOUSEHOLD

This is by far the largest department in the Royal Household with over 250 men and women employed in a variety of jobs from kitchen porter and footman to Palace Steward.

Every meal, every room, every function held at Buckingham Palace and Windsor Castle, and at Balmoral, the Palace of Holyroodhouse and Sandringham comes directly under his responsibility.

Air Vice-Marshal (now Air Marshal) Sir David Walker is the current Master of the Household. In 2011, in addition to his £120,000 salary, he was given the added bonus of being created a Knight of the Royal Victorian Order, so he is now Sir David.

Within his bailiwick are five sub-divisions: 'G' (General) Branch, which looks after the entertainment and ceremonial side of the Palace; 'F' (Food Branch is responsible for preparing and cooking and, most importantly, presentation of the food at the royal tables – and for the Household; 'H' (Housekeeping) Branch maintains the cleaning of all the royal residences. If the Chief Housekeeper decides some of the sheets on The Queen's bed should be replaced, she has to obtain the permission of the Master of the Household before she can buy new ones. He then has to ask the Keeper of the Privy Purse for the money. 'C' (Craft) Branch includes the upholsterers, French polishers and other craftsmen who are on constant call to restore, repair and conserve the valuable furniture at every royal home from their base at Windsor Castle. If a cushion, carpet or pair of curtains needs repair, then it is 'C' Branch who are called on to undertake the job. A seamstress at Windsor Castle once spent days sewing the ends of a pair of curtains after a couple of the Corgis had chewed their way through and tried to swing on them – all without once being scolded. Then there is the Central Office, which arranges, with the office of the Lord Chamberlain, the guest lists and seating plans at official events such as a State Banquet. This can be quite a headache when arranging seating plans at which certain individuals are on the 'must-have' guest list and the office is besieged with requests from members of the Household, who will also be attending, not to sit next to a particular man or woman.

The Ladies-in-Waiting used to plead with the office not to put them near the late Ted Heath, the former Prime Minister, who was regarded as the most boring dinner guest ever seen at the Palace. Heath was uncomfortable with women – and not much better with men – and several of the Ladies said they had spent an entire formal meal sitting next to him without him uttering a single word to them.

With a staff of over 250, it requires an administration team to coordinate the management of the department and the Chief Clerk is the man with day-to-day responsibility for the hundred and one details that go into the planning and preparation, including the 600 or so meals a day provided for the Royal Household. The Chief Clerk is paid around £30,000 a year. If he did the same job in one of London's top hotels, he would earn at least twice that amount.

When young men and women join the Master of the Household's Department as trainee footmen – and they call the females footmen – they are introduced to a rigorous training scheme, starting with a section entitled Waiting at Table. There are periods of specific instruction beginning Introduction to the Dining Room, Reading of Orders, Reading of Menus, Appearance and Behaviour, followed by lessons in the Types of Plates and how they should be handled and the Order and Continuity of the Meals. A vital part of their training concerns the Handling of Food: Main Dishes, Vegetable Dishes and Sauce Boats. Then comes Serving Dessert, Serving Coffee and finally Clearing the Dining Room. The above sections are all explained in initial upper case in the written orders of the Deputy Master of the Household. The trainees are tested at specific times, before being given an assessment of proficiency and finally, when they have satisfied the Sergeant Footman a record signed by their trainer is placed in their personnel file.

The nest stage of their training involves duties in the cellars, where they learn how to open bottles of wine, how to decant it and how to recognise different types of glasses and which should be used for particular drinks. Their final section is lessons in how to serve wine at table and at cocktail parties.

THE LORD CHAMBERLAIN'S OFFICE

Considering the Lord Chamberlain is the Head of the Royal Household, he has very little to do with the day-to-day running of the department that bears his name.

The Comptroller of the Lord Chamberlain's Office is the man with that responsibility and in an organisation like the Royal Household, where attention to detail is taken for granted, this office is where it all begins and ends.

Every investiture at Buckingham Palace, as well as the single one held at the Palace of Holyroodhouse and one other at Cardiff Castle, is the responsibility of the Comptroller. All the ceremonial arrangements come under his jurisdiction and on a personal level, he is the man who instructs those who are about to be honoured, in the way they should conduct themselves. More than one soon-to-be knight has cause to thank the Comptroller for the courteous and humorous way in which he has guided them through the labyrinth of the protocol when they stand before The Queen waiting for the sword to descend on their shoulder.

He even shows the ladies how to curtsy and if they laugh at him, all the better. He knows it is one way to get them relaxed before they enter the State Ballroom.

Lt Col. Andrew Ford, the current Comptroller, is one of the most popular heads of department and his staff are always prepared to go that extra mile on his behalf.

Considering he is the lowest paid of the top six, just scraping into the six figure category on £101,000 a year, there doesn't seem to be any logic in having him controlling the department whose activities are the most seen by the public and the media.

In recent years one of the most recognisable Comptrollers was Lieutenant Colonel Sir John Johnston, of the Grenadier Guards. Known as Johnnie to his colleagues and every member of the Royal Family, he served in the Lord Chamberlain's office for more than twenty years and in 1981 at the wedding of the Prince of Wales and Lady Diana Spencer, it was the splendid figure of Johnnie, in scarlet uniform, who was seen by millions on television handing the soon-to-be Princess of Wales from the Glass Coach onto the steps of St Paul's Cathedral.

He later told me that it was one of the proudest days of his life. He also said that when they returned to Buckingham Palace the Princess kissed him on the cheek and thanked him for all he had done. In his twenty years at the Palace no one had ever done that before and he wasn't sure which had given him the greater shock: the kiss or being shouted at by the sergeant major when he first entered Sandhurst as a cadet officer.

One of the most intriguing parts of the Comptroller's department is a tiny office located above a former dungeon in St James's Palace where just eleven people work.

Its full title is Central Chancery of the Orders of Knighthood and this is where the secrets are kept of who is to be awarded a knighthood. Twice a year the New Year's Honours List and The Queen's Birthday Honours List are published and it is here that the names and decorations are finalised. When you realise that with twenty-two investitures held at Buckingham Palace every year, plus those in Edinburgh and Cardiff, to which up to 150 men and women are invited, the total number of OBEs, MBEs, CBEs and all the other awards amounts to a staggering 3,000 medals with each one attached to its own distinctive ribbon and placed in its own leather box.

The attention to detail is meticulous. No mistakes are permitted. Though there was one hilarious occasion when someone dropped a cushion holding a number of awards during an investiture ceremony in the State Ballroom. The Queen solved the problem saying, 'Just put them any way you can. I'll give them anything and you can sort it out afterwards.' So a gentleman who was expecting to be made a Commander of the British Empire, found that for a few minutes at least, he had been demoted to a mere MBE. While a lady who had been told she was to be awarded the most junior level found she had been elevated to the highest – for the moment it took to get her back to the side room where it was indeed all sorted out. Her Majesty's reaction had never been revealed, but it was she who saved the day – and the red faces of her staff. Throughout the entire incident she didn't turn a hair and just carried on as if nothing had happened. That's what fifty years of royal training had achieved.

When one realises how long the Honours system has been in operation, it is hard to imagine the numbers involved when Central Chancery say they have the names and dates of every recipient of every award going back to 1348 when King Edward III founded the Order of the Garter.

The Comptroller's office also makes a healthy profit for the Crown as guests and recipients at Investitures are not allowed to bring cameras or videos inside the Palace. Instead, a team of professional photographers and cameramen are contracted to provide copies of the entire proceedings, with the individual being honoured inserted, at a cost of around £120 plus £25 for a set of still photographs. As nearly everyone takes advantage of the offers it is not too difficult to do the sums.

St James's Palace is a warren of hidden courts and alleys where different members of the Royal Family live and where several departments of the Household have their offices. A section of the Lord Chamberlain's Office is based in Ambassador's Court. It is the post of Marshal of the Diplomatic Corps who arranges for all Ambassadors and High Commissioners to be collected from their residences when they are due to present their credentials to The Queen. Together with the Crown Equerry, the Marshal, who is always a retired military officer of senior rank, makes sure the incoming emissary knows that he or she is required to do when they meet Her Majesty for the first time, and that they are aware that although the ceremony invariably takes place in the morning, full evening dress is mandatory.

The Marshal also assures every diplomat that the size and importance of their country makes no difference to The Queen and the way in which they are received. Everyone gets the same treatment – large or small. He knows how important it is for representatives of smaller countries not to feel patronised. A horse-drawn carriage is sent to the residence, for the ambassador or High Commissioner, with cars to bring family members and others who are to be presented. The audience lasts for exactly the same period and The Queen is punctilious in observing the correct procedure for each one.

The Marshal also arranges for diplomats to attend Royal Ascot (in the Royal Enclosure), Garden Parties (where they take their tea in the Royal Marquee) and the most important social event of the year, the Diplomatic Reception which is held in Buckingham Palace every November. This is when he is required to know and be able to recognise every guest in the room, as he has to present them individually to Her Majesty.

The Comptroller of the Lord Chamberlain's Office has several other ceremonial responsibilities. Each year two incoming State Visits are made by foreign Heads of State and the Comptroller makes all the arrangements, from which member of the Royal Family meets the visitor and conducts them to the Palace (The Queen never travels to airports to greet her guests), to the hoisting of the correct flags along The Mall, and the Guard of Honour in the Forecourt of Buckingham Palace.

And when The Queen attends the State Opening of Parliament, her Comptroller of the Lord Chamberlain's Office, with his colleague from the Royal Mews (part of his office) arranges the processional details.

Many of his responsibilities go back several centuries, but the attention to detail is as meticulous today as it has ever been. There's only one standard – perfection.

THE CROWN EQUERRY

When Prince Charles and Princess Anne were very young, The Queen decided that they should learn to ride. It was almost as soon as they could walk. The man given the task was the then Crown Equerry, Lt Col Sir John Miller, a retired officer of the Welsh Guards.

John Miller was a shy, introspective bachelor who was totally devoted to The Queen and her family. He was also an expert horseman, in spite of the fact that he belonged to a regiment of foot guards and not the cavalry. He had already introduced the Duke of Edinburgh to carriage driving when arthritis forced him to give up his favourite equestrian sport of polo.

The riding lessons were carried out in the Mews riding school which is seventy-five yards long, so there's plenty of room to learn to canter. The surface of the school is laid over a six-foot-deep foundation of faggots and peat and when Charles and Anne – and later Andrew and Edward – were learning to ride, loud music would be played from loudspeakers to teach them how to control the beasts if they were out and a military band marched by.

Lieutenant Colonel Miller spent more than a quarter of a century in royal service and working from the Royal Mews, he declared it his personal fiefdom, and even members of the Royal Family deferred to him in transport matters, especially anything to do with horses as he unreservedly expressed his own preference for horsepower to be on four legs rather than under the bonnet of a car.

His greatest pride was his punctuality. He claimed, with every justification, that no royal engagement with which he was involved, ever ran late, even by a minute.

He was therefore horrified when, on the eve of the wedding of the Prince of Wales and Lady Diana Spencer in 1981, the bride-to-be informed him that she wished to exercise the bride's traditional prerogative and arrive at St Paul's Cathedral a few minutes behind the scheduled time. The Colonel had been over the route many times, stopwatch in hand, even instructing soldiers to throw buckets of water in front of the horses hooves so they would know what to expect if it rained on the day.

The timetables had been printed and distributed to everyone involved, including the media. Miller knew that if he obeyed the soon-to-be Princess of Wales his reputation for punctuality would be in tatters. He spoke to colleagues in the Household, including the Lord Chamberlain, who refused to become involved. He eventually asked The Queen what he should do – and this was only hours before the ceremony was due to start. Her Majesty told him to compromise and that's what he did.

When Diana arrived at St Paul's she was seen to be just thirty seconds late. Nobody remarked on the fact and though Sir John was not entirely placated, both sides felt that honour had been satisfied and Diana gave him a kiss when she returned to the Palace, much to the dismay of her new husband who felt the gesture was taking things a bit too far.

Sir John Miller had a niece who was quite well proportioned and, like him, an excellent rider. In the days when The Queen rode Burmese, a black Canadian mare, in the annual Sovereign's Birthday Parade (Trooping the Colour), the niece would ride Burmese for several hours before the parade to tire her a little so that there was no danger of the horse becoming too frisky when The Queen, who was, and remains, an excellent horsewoman, was on board.

The Crown Equerry lives during his tenure of office in a magnificent three-storey residence just inside the entrance to the Royal Mews in Buckingham Palace Road. The property is far too big for the average family, almost impossible to heat and the Equerry has to rely on the Royal Collection to help furnish the place as the rooms are so large, most modern furniture would be lost in them.

In Queen Victoria's day, her Crown Equerry lived in the house in great splendour, with ten hot and cold running servants, all paid for by her. Today, one part-time cleaner is employed. No cook, no footmen and no housemaids. Only one thing has remained and that is the original black cast iron cooking oven in the basement kitchen. It hasn't been used for generations. But it is so large and heavy; said to be over two tons, it cannot be moved. So it remains an unseen museum piece.

In addition to his responsibilities in the Royal Mews, the present Crown Equerry has recently been given the job of Director of Royal Travel, which means he now looks after air travel and the Royal Train as well as transport by horse, carriage and motor car. As there is no longer a dedicated Queen's Flight, the Royal Family's flying is now undertaken by No.32 (The Royal Squadron) based at RAF Northolt in West London. But this is not used exclusively by the Royal Family. The squadron also handles flights made by Government ministers.

THE ROYAL COLLECTION

The Royal Household has had its fair share of rogues in the past but none compares with the man The Queen had trusted with millions of pounds worth of art from the Royal Collection, her Surveyor of The Queen's Pictures, Sir Anthony Blunt KCVO. Blunt was a spy, and had been in the pay of the Russians since the 1930s, and was a member of the Cambridge Five, a group of brilliant undergraduates, who included the notorious Guy Burgess, Kim Philby and Donald Maclean, who were recruited to work for Russia and did so until they were uncovered sometime in the 1950s.

Blunt was one of those brilliant academics from Oxbridge who was persuaded that Communism and the Soviet system were preferable to the capitalist society of the western world. Yet, he refused to go and live in the East, even when ordered by his KGB masters, and enjoyed a comfortable lifestyle working in the Royal Household establishing a reputation as one of the world's leading art experts.

His credentials were impeccable. Apart from his academic qualifications, he was also a third cousin of The Queen Mother, so he was socially at home in royal circles.

After he had been unmasked as a Soviet spy, it was revealed that as long ago as 1948 he was suspected of working against Britain. Sir Alan (Tommy) Lascelles, King George VI's private secretary, was heard to refer to Blunt as 'our Russian spy'. But nobody did anything about him during this period.

Blunt confessed to his spying activities in 1964, and The Queen was informed. However, she decided to keep him in his job, and in return for his confession, and the fact that he had given the names of several of his fellow spies; he was granted immunity from prosecution.

It wasn't until 1979, fifteen years after his confession that his role was finally revealed. The Queen then stripped him of his knighthood and to add to his humiliation he was asked to resign from his clubs, the Athenaeum and the Travellers, much to his dismay.

Blunt's boss in the Royal Collection was Kenneth [later Lord] Clark, who was to achieve great acclaim as the presenter of the television series *Civilisation*. He was also known as the father of Alan Clark, Member of Parliament, friend of Margaret Thatcher, serial womaniser and the most outrageous diarist – the Boswell of his generation.

With an estimated total of over a million items in the Royal Collection, including the finest collection of Fabergé eggs in existence, there are paintings, drawings, engravings, sculptures, furniture and other priceless *objets d'art* in what is certainly the most important private art collection in the world.

It is also the department in the Royal Household that consistently shows a profit for The Queen. The Collection grants reproduction rights to a wide range of commercial interests: book and magazine publishers, television companies including the BBC and others throughout the world.

Every time a photograph of one of The Queen's pictures or other works of art appears anywhere in the world (nowhere is exempt), it is stipulated that the words 'With Her Majesty's Gracious Permission' are included. It is also part of the deal that a fee must be paid to the Royal Collection on behalf of The Queen.

The Collection maintains some 2,500 colour transparencies; applications for black and white are diminishing, with more being added every year. It is truly big business, with the sums involved running to hundreds of thousands of pounds as the men and women who organise this section all know this is very much a seller's market. If customers want something from The Queen's collection, this is the only place they can go.

Another aspect of the work of the Royal Collection is the loan of valuable works of art to outside organisations from time to time. When something that may be worth millions, is borrowed, those on the receiving end have to fulfil a number of stringent conditions such as insurance, transport and the security of the building where the work is being displayed. The insurance premiums are prohibitive in many cases, and there is an experienced specialist transport company that carries all Royal Collection items throughout the United Kingdom. The paperwork is vast and the formalities complex when anything is borrowed.

There is also a body called the Royal Palaces Exhibition Committee, which is responsible for mounting all the displays of royal treasures that change annually in The Queen's Gallery at Buckingham Palace and those at other royal palaces.

When some of The Queen's dresses were exhibited at Buckingham Palace it involved not only the experts from the Collection, but Her Majesty's personal assistant, Angela Kelly, with the final approval coming from The Queen herself.

Money pours into the Royal Collection from a wide variety of sources. The profits from admissions to the Windsor Castle State Apartments, Queen Mary's Dolls House, the exhibition of Old Master Drawings, The Queen's Gallery at Buckingham Palace, entrance to the Royal Mews, as well as the takings from all the shops in royal residences, go into something called the Royal Palaces Presentation Fund. This Fund is administered by the Keeper of the Privy Purse, with the Director of the Royal Collection, the Superintendent of Public Enterprises, the Deputy Treasurer to The Queen and the Financial Controller of the Royal Palaces Presentation Fund forming the management committee.

Like any other consumer-oriented business, all sorts of conditions affect their takings. If the weather is too hot, or too wet, the customers don't come. If there is a transport strike in the UK or just in London, takings will drop off. Bomb threats and political upheaval can also cause difficulties and have implications in that the Director of the Royal Collection is only able to buy new items or spend money available for repairs and restoration work, if it comes from the profits.

All the shops in the royal palaces, especially Buckingham Palace sell souvenirs at prices that tourists are delighted to pay and the Royal Collection uses the latest retail practices to make sure that only the best sellers are stocked.

Some current examples are: fine bone china from the Royal Collection, including a Queen Victoria Tankard at £30, a Windsor Castle Garter Mug at £12.95, an Imperial Russian Yellow Pillbox Clock at £49, a Buckingham Palace Guardsman Childs Mug at £9.95. At Sandringham, Staffordshire pottery is always a best seller with a Sandringham Blue on White Mug at £7.99 very popular with visitors.

At Balmoral, where admission prices are £8.70 for adults with seniors (over sixty) receiving a concession of £1 and children under sixteen paying just £4.60, visitors are allowed only until 31 July each year, because after that The Queen will be in residence and no one gets in while she is at home.

Being in the Highlands of Scotland, the gift shop offers, in addition to the usual items, Balmoral Malt Whisky distilled at Royal Lochnagar for £12.95 or a special bottle of 70cl at £34.99.

The most recent Royal Wedding, that of the Duke and Duchess of Cambridge, gave a welcome impetus to the royal retail trade with a set of five postcards costing £4 up to a William and Catherine Cushion in blue velvet embroidered with the couples' initials and the date of the wedding. This sells for £85 and to tempt the thousands of American tourists who pay to see around the Palace in the summer months, the prices are converted into US dollars.

When they were trying to decide what items to sell containing the initials of the Duke and Duchess, those in charge of the retail outlets agonised for weeks over whether to use 'W' and 'C' or 'W' and 'K' as most people, still refer to the new Duchess as Kate. They finally opted for 'C' for Catherine, but obviously the letters WC have another meaning in Britain and the powers-that-be were concerned that the couple might become the butt of crude jokes.

In all the royal bookshops, the biggest seller by far is a slim volume dedicated to the memory of the late Diana, Princess of Wales. It also happens to be one of the cheapest selling for £6.99. When the book was first published in 1997, to mark Diana's death, it was expected to sell just a couple of thousand copies as her memory faded. It hasn't happened and the wedding of William and Catherine has meant a resurgence of interest in William's mother, so the book just goes on selling.

Across the road from Clarence House is Marlborough House where a Furniture Restoration Workshop is located in the Mews. The men and women employed here are all skilled craftspeople on a par with their opposite numbers at the Victoria and Albert Museum, said to be the best in the world.

Where valuable furniture is concerned their biggest enemy is central heating, which can cause wood to expand, contract and splinter. So the restorers are working throughout the year trying to keep pace with the demands of the Master of the Household, who is responsible for everything inside all the royal residences.

In an organisation as large as the Royal Household there are little accidents inevitably. A young housemaid once knocked over a magnificent – and expensive – Sevres vase breaking it into several pieces. She was terrified that if anyone found out she would be sacked, so she tried to mend it herself with superglue. Of course, it didn't work and at first she didn't reveal that she was to blame.

The problem was that the restorers, when they at last saw the damage, didn't know what material had been used in the botched repair. Eventually the Master of the Household called an amnesty as long as the culprit owned up. The girl came forward and told the restorers what she had tried to do. They then set about dismantling the vase and painstakingly putting it back together. They were successful. But it took two years before it could be replaced in its place of honour in one of the State Apartments. The Queen was kept informed of events and she ordered that the maid, who had owned up, should not be dismissed and at the last count she was still working in the Palace.

Nearly every member of the Royal Family enjoys art in some shape or form and the Director of the Royal Collection advises him or her when he or she intends to make a purchase.

It doesn't always work out as a former Director found out when he told the late Queen Mother not to buy the work of an artist she discovered. It was

John Piper who Queen Elizabeth thought was an excellent war artist, but the Director thought he was not all that commercial. Her Majesty disagreed and bought a number of his paintings including a squadron of RAF fighter planes who had been based on Smith's Lawn at Windsor Castle during the Second World War.

Queen Elizabeth paid just a few hundred pounds for the majority of the paintings she bought. It was a pretty sound investment. Today they are worth over £50,000 each. So, her philosophy that you should buy what you like, not what an expert tells you to buy, proved to be the right one.

There are all sorts of tiny sub-divisions in the Royal Collection; one of the smallest is the clock-winding section consisting of just two men who are employed to wind and maintain the 300 clocks in Buckingham Palace, as well as those in Windsor Castle. The men know all the shortcuts between rooms and their busiest time is when they have to advance and later retard the clocks in March when summer time is announced and then put back to normal time in October. The horologists used to come under the jurisdiction of the Master of the Household, but it was discovered that most of the clocks are not merely timepieces but extremely valuable. Some were specially commissioned by past sovereigns, including one that was bought by Henry VIII for Anne Boleyn with the original account of three pounds still in pristine condition. Therefore it was thought appropriate to transfer the responsibility to the Surveyor of The Queen's Works of Art, so they now work for him.

As with every department within the Royal Household, the future of the Royal Collection depends on money and how much becomes available. The Queen is no longer able to buy anything she wants. There isn't a bottomless purse any more. Russian, Chinese and Middle-Eastern billionaires can easily outbid Her Majesty when it comes to buying new works of art. And when economies have to be made, the Royal Collection department becomes vulnerable, as other offices are able to prove their requirements should take priority.

It is only by increasing the number and variety of the exhibitions the Palace mounts that this dedicated band of vastly experienced men and women can continue to devote their working lives to the preservation of the most important private art collection in the world.

Art is now a worldwide business and the Royal Collection is looking far beyond the United Kingdom boundaries to expand its exhibition arm.

They believe – and The Queen agrees – that art is to be shared by everyone, not just those who can afford it.

CHAPTER SEVEN

VALETS – OR GENTLEMEN'S GENTLEMEN

Valets have to be invisible; that is merge into the background and only be there as and when required. But there are occasions when the utmost intimacy – and discretion is needed. When Prince Charles's 'Honorary' Grandfather, the late Earl Mountbatten of Burma, rode alongside The Queen at the annual Birthday Parade (Trooping the Colour) his Life Guard breeches were so tight-fitting that his valet, William Evans, had to sprinkle talcum powder inside the legs and along his thighs, in order to force his legs in. And once the uniform had been donned, it was impossible to sit down – or go to the loo. And when the parade was over the process had to be carried out in reverse, which was even more difficult and unpleasant, as Lord Mountbatten's legs had become sweaty in the extreme from sitting on

155

horseback for several hours. However, neither master nor servant found anything unusual in being involved in such a delicate situation, which was repeated year after year.

As footmen are often called upon to act as valets to members of the Royal Family and their guests, their training scheme also includes detailed instructions on valeting, beginning with how to identify and lay out civilian dress: Morning Coat, Dinner Jacket, Household Coat, Windsor Coat and White Tie.

Under the section, Care of Clothes, they learn how to press suits and uniforms (nothing is ever sent to a dry cleaner). Sponge and hand press is the way a gentleman's gentleman always handles his master's clothes. They also have weeks of instruction in the art of cleaning boots and shoes and uniform accessories, and packing and unpacking clothes.

A note on valeting duties explains that the aim of a valet should be to know the personal requirements of the gentleman he is valeting and to work unobtrusively to provide the services necessary.

The would-be valet is also advised that no two gentlemen will want to be valeted in exactly the same way, but the following general guidelines should be observed.

When unpacking a case, the valet should remember that suitcases have been put down on 'filthy' station platforms and on pavements and roads… therefore it is a crime to put them on clean valuable bed covers.

Collars, ties and handkerchiefs should be placed in the top drawer of the dressing table. Socks should also be in an easily accessible place.

When hanging suits in wardrobes (especially when they are very close together) make sure that sleeves are hanging straight, particularly the sleeves nearest the back of the wardrobe.

When removing clothes for valeting the following rules should be followed:

Garments must only be removed when they need attention. For example, a hairy tweed jacket may not need pressing or brushing.

Empty all pockets before removing clothes and when carrying a suit in one hand and a pair of shoes in the other, it is a crime to hold the shoes against the clothes as the soles may have picked up traces of dirt and engine oil, while the uppers will have polish on them. A good valet carries a supply of bags to place shoes in just in case.

Always leave a gentleman's braces on the trousers and never take away his cufflinks. Leave them on the dressing table.

There are also strict instructions on how to awake your gentleman in the morning:

Open the door as quietly as possible. Do not shine a light in the gentleman's eyes. Draw back the curtains and gather up the evening clothes (guests always dress for dinner at Buckingham Palace and Windsor Castle) in this order: Jacket first, then the trousers, in their creases, shirt and underclothes. Tuck the socks and bow tie inside one of the shoes so they won't be lost on the way to the pressing room.

Next draw a bath, having tested the temperature of the water, but close the connecting door in order not to disturb the gentleman. And always remember to pour a little hot water into the bath before filling it, as baths can be cold and you do not want your gentleman to be uncomfortable when he sits down for the first time.

The instructions continue. 'Up to now you have not spoken. This is as it should be. However, once you have laid out the outfit for the morning, tell the gentleman the time and what the weather is like and then leave the room quietly carrying his evening clothes.'

The valet will have already brought the 'Calling Tray' when he wakes the gentleman. Tea or coffee in bone china cups (no mugs are used in royal residences) and biscuits, on a silver tray.

There is an instruction, of course, in the Removal of the Tray. It states: Remove the tray as soon as possible after the gentleman has gone to breakfast. Also tidy the room and put away the dressing gown, pyjamas and slippers. Only very elderly guests are served breakfast in bed.

Getting the guest ready for evening entertainment is a ritual in itself that has to be strictly adhered to.

A good valet will always undo the buttons on an evening shirt so that it will be ready for him to slip on. If the shirt is wrapped in laundry paper and cardboard, remove them and throw them in the wastebasket.

If collar studs are required, put them in, so the gentleman won't have to fiddle with them himself.

The final instruction with evening clothes, after a careful brushing, is to imagine you are dressing yourself, and then you won't forget anything.

And if you think all that is enough to be going on with, Here's the drill when a valet is helping a military member of the Royal Household get dressed for a ceremonial duty such as the Trooping the Colour or State Opening of Parliament.

This is the order in which formal uniforms are to be laid out. Scarlet tunic, Overall Trouser, Boots and Spurs, Gold Sash, Aiguillettes, Sword Belt, Gold Sword Slings, Sword with gold knot, Large medals, White collarless shirt, bear-skin cap, white kid gloves.

The valet then has to learn the method of laying out.

Attach the Aiguillettes and the medals to the tunic and hang it on a chest of drawers. Box the overalls and place them in front of a chair. Place the folded shirt on the chair, remembering the cufflinks. Lay the remainder of the accessories: the sword, sword belt and the sash on the bed. Leave the bearskin on its stand in a prominent place (it's hardly likely to get lost) and place the gloves on the bed.

Further instructions remind the valet that the medal, spurs and tunic buttons must be polished, with the welts of the boots being polished even if the boots themselves are patent. The white piping on the tunic should be whitened with chalk, but only under the supervision of the Sergeant Footman or his Deputy. The sword scabbard must be rubbed up with a soft cloth.

There are separate sets of instructions for the uniforms worn at different formal functions.

The U.1 Ceremonial (worn for new High Commissioners and Ambassadors presenting their credentials at Buckingham Palace) means the scarlet tunic is replaced with a blue one and the instruction contains the message that the overall straps should be fastened as tightly as possible under the instep.

When the Prime Minister has his weekly audience of The Queen every Tuesday evening at 6.30 p.m., the officer on duty wears a blue frock coat with a crimson sash, the same outfit he wears when in attendance at an Investiture.

For outside engagements that are regarded as 'lounge suit' affairs the officer wears Khaki service dress complete with Sam Brown Belt, which has to be spit and polished to an immaculate sheen. The valet is advised to clean the brass work first, rather than risk getting Duraglit over the polished leather. And when laying out this uniform, put the jacket over the back of a chair, the trousers on the seat of the chair, with the shirt on top. Then place the shoes by the side of the chair with the folded socks on top of the shoes. The tie should be placed on the dressing table.

When all this has been done and the clothes have to be put away until the next time, a good valet knows that wet shoes should never be dried in excessive heat, as more than one enthusiastic youngster has found to his cost when he has placed wet shoes in the oven to dry them quickly and found they have cracked.

The ideal way is to stuff old newspapers inside the shoes and let them dry naturally. It takes longer but it preserves the leather. Once they are dry, shoetrees must be inserted and the shoes carefully polished by hand before they are put away.

The next chore is to press the clothes that have been worn. As the Deputy Master of the Household says in his instructions, 'No Savile Row tailor would dream of sending out a suit or jacket with creases in the sleeves.' So when pressing a gentleman's coat valets must use the sleeve bolsters, and lapels should always be pressed from the back to give a 'roll' effect.

Trousers should not be over pressed as this gives a 'too sharp' appearance – perhaps a bit like a second-hand car salesman.

Under garments should, whenever possible, be washed by hand with the water not too hot.

If a footman is valeting a gentleman who is leaving the Palace after a visit, he should make sure all his personal belongings are packed (there is a detailed instruction in how to pack and unpack, in what order and telling the valet how much tissue paper should be used) and he should be on hand for any last-minute requirements. Overnight visitors are told that tipping is neither expected nor acceptable. However, if the valeting has been of particularly fine quality, it would be a churlish guest who didn't press a £20 note into a waiting hand when he leaves. And if he didn't, the word would quickly get around among the rest of the staff – before the next visit.

CHAPTER EIGHT

GUARDING ROYALTY

P rince Charles once asked his personal protection officer how much he was paying him. When the man replied, 'Absolutely nothing, Sir,' Charles was amazed and, at first delighted, as he thought he was getting his protection without having to put his hand in his own pocket. Which was true. None of the Royal Family pays for their police officers, which is just as well as they earn a great deal more than most of the men and women employed in the Household, and the Royals would hate to think they were paying the salaries of these dedicated officers.

Because the bodyguards of The Queen and her family are seen alongside their charges dressed in immaculate suits that could have come straight from Savile Row, many people think they are detectives or secret service agents. In fact, every one of them is a member of the uniformed branch of 'A' Division of the Metropolitan Police, and part of the Royalty and Diplomatic Department that protects not only the Royal Family, but also every foreign emissary in London and the Prime Minister and other Government ministers and officials.

And even though they remain in the uniformed branch of the service they carry out their duties in plain clothes, for which they receive a generous allowance.

The only police officers who wear their uniforms on duty are those guarding the gates at Buckingham Palace, St James's Palace, Clarence House and every other royal residence, and the men and women who work in the police post.

The constables on the gates, who these days are armed, earn between £22,680 and £35,610 a year depending on length of service, while the sergeant who supervises them is on a salary scale of £35,610– £40,020. It is a sergeant who sits outside The Queen's bedroom throughout the night, unarmed and wearing slippers so she won't be disturbed.

The lowest rank of plain-clothes bodyguard is Sergeant, with most of them Inspectors earning between £47,625 and £51,504.

When they are promoted to Chief Inspector, they can expect to see their salary increased to a minimum of £52,578 up to a maximum of £54,588.

On reaching the rank of Superintendent, they start to make serious money. £60,750 rising by £10,000 eventually to £70,779 and the man who is The Queen's principal protection officer, a Chief Superintendent, starts on £72,543, which can rise to £76,680.

All these salaries are in line with the pay scale for police officers working in the Metropolitan area, so those who guard, for example, Gatcombe Park in Gloucestershire, the home of the Princess Royal, or Raymill House, the private home of the Duchess of Cornwall, which is fully manned throughout the year even though she rarely visits it, are paid at the lower end of the pay scales.

So you can see why Prince Charles was pleased to hear that he didn't have to pay his bodyguards. The thought that they earned more than his personal staff would have appalled him.

Most personal protection officers remain with the Royal Family for years. Occasionally they will be moved from one member to another, sometimes because they simply don't get on and the Royal has asked for the officer to be moved, or the policeman or woman, just prefers to work elsewhere. Princess Margaret once had a man removed because of what she complained was his B.O. She didn't say this was the reason, merely that they were incompatible, but when he moved to another royal lady, who also disliked his body odour, he was quickly relegated to a job miles away from royalty, and everyone knew the real reason.

An otherwise excellent officer who had passed the initial test fell at the last fence through no fault of his own. It was that he had a disfiguring birthmark on his face. The Royals wouldn't have minded; they probably wouldn't even have noticed, but the senior officers conducting the final phase of the examination realised that the officer would stand out and as anonymity is paramount in Royal Protection, this man was returned to his unit, where he later distinguished himself and rose to high rank within the police force.

The late Diana, Princess of Wales, was protected for years by Ken Warfe, who has since achieved celebrity status as a television pundit. Mr Warfe was very popular with the Princess and her staff and when he moved from her side it was because she decided, after her divorce, not to continue with royal protection. It is freely acknowledged that if she had retained her official bodyguards, she would not have been in that car in Paris on the night she died; they would not have allowed it.

The junior officers are usually attached to the younger members of the Royal Family, as they often have to stay up late when the Royals go clubbing in London and abroad. When Prince William was single, he and his brother Harry, would often remain at a nightclub until three or four in the morning, and no matter how late it was, the bodyguards had to stay at their side. The younger officers didn't mind too much, as it meant they were racking up stacks of overtime.

When Princesses Beatrice and Eugenie had official bodyguards, they too were late birds. However, because of the public outcry at the cost of their protection, said to be around £500,000 a year, it was withdrawn in 2010, much to the dismay of their father, the Duke of York, who protested to The Queen. Her Majesty, who normally cannot refuse her children anything, agreed with the recommendations of her Private Secretary, who had been told by the police authorities that they did not consider the Princesses to be at risk, and the protection ended.

Neither Peter nor Zara Phillips, children of the Princess Royal and as much The Queen's grandchildren as any of the others, has ever had police protection, and Princess Anne has never believed it was necessary.

When her children were tiny they were often seen in the grounds at Gatcombe being carried on the shoulders of one of the policemen, but that was only because their mother was nearby and it was her they were protecting. Several visitors to Gatcombe Park remarked on the apparent closeness of the Phillips children to the police officers, but when it was mentioned to one of them, he dismissed the idea with a laugh saying the children had been taught practically from birth to regard them as just another part of their mother's staff. Even Peter and Zara, the only grandchildren of The Queen not to have titles, were brought up never to become too close to the servants.

There is one disadvantage to remaining too long in royal service; it is that promotion is slow. To move up the ladder, police officers need to obtain experience in other branches of the service. But the majority of those who work at the Palace, and other residences, like the work, enjoy the extensive travel, with generous expenses, and apart from the occasional hassle, it is not too demanding.

Of course, they will always point out that one of their number, James Beaton, who served as personal protection officer to Princess Anne when she was first married, was shot five times as he tried to protect her from an attempted kidnapping in The Mall in 1974. His gallantry earned him a George Cross and the undying gratitude of The Queen and Prince Philip in saving their only daughter's life. He didn't get any monetary reward for his bravery, apart from the £100 a year annuity that is paid to all holders of the GC. Jim Beaton went on to become The Queen's personal protection officer for nine years and since his retirement he has remained on excellent terms with Her Majesty and Their Royal Highnesses.

The man in charge of Royal Protection is a Commander of 'A' Division, whose headquarters is at Cannon Row Police Station, but who usually operates from a special police station built in the grounds of Buckingham Palace, discreetly hidden behind The Queen's Gallery, at a cost of £1.6 million in 1982. This was shortly following the arrest of Michael Fagan, the man who was found in The Queen's bedroom one morning when she woke up.

The money did not come from the Royal Household budget but was entirely financed by the police and Home Office.

The police post – they do not call it a station – is completely shielded from public view and is hidden beneath a mound of earth and grass behind a group of fully mature trees. It is difficult to see, even from the Palace windows.

Inside, the post is equipped with a very high-tech radio communications centre from where they are able to track the movements of every royal vehicle that leaves the Palace. There is also a canteen, even though the men and women on duty prefer to eat in the staff servery, where they say the food is better. There is a map room, briefing room and separate changing rooms for those who work on Palace security. But there is no bar. Neither are there any cells. If anyone needs to be detained they are driven over to Cannon Row station.

The Police post has its own fully equipped underground garage as police cars are not housed in the Royal Mews with the rest of the royal fleet, and the men and women who guard the Royals do not like leaving their private cars on the forecourt as some members of the Household are allowed to do.

A Chief Superintendent commands the Royalty, Special Patrol and Special Escort Motorcycle Group; these are the outriders you see on their high-powered motorbikes, who ride ahead of any royal cars, making sure no one gets in the way and 'figuratively' ensuring that all lights turn to green.

A uniformed Chief Inspector runs the Control Room, just inside the Side Entrance to Buckingham Palace, which is connected to the Palace itself, and every other royal residence. So if an incident occurs at say, Highgrove House or Kensington Palace or Bagshot House, the control room is aware immediately and the machine moves rapidly into action. They also have one other link not usually discussed in open conversation. They are in direct touch with SAS headquarters in Hereford, with a system of secret code words related to the seriousness of any incident.

Every police officer attached to royalty is a volunteer and they have to be recommended by their divisional senior officer before they are subjected to the most rigorous selection process. The slightest blemish on their record means they go no farther but once they do pass the tests, and before they take up their posts, they attend a special course at the Hendon Police Driving School training them in handling cars at high speed.

They also learn the rudiments of emergency medical treatment, and strange as it may seem, have lessons in etiquette and social skills. They have to be comfortable in the surroundings that are the norm with their royal charges, so they need to be able to wear morning clothes for Royal Ascot, weddings and funerals, and dinner jackets for formal evening functions. In addition, their clothes, both for men and women, need to be fairly loose fitting, to accommodate their shoulder holsters. It is not difficult to pick them out when the Royals are out and about as the bodyguards are usually the only ones with their coats open – again to make it easy for them to reach their guns.

When an officer is accepted for royal duty he or she spends the first six months shadowing one of the others before being allocated to one of the family. They are moved around quite a bit to see how they fit in and they may be chosen personally by one of the Princes or Princesses. They are never asked directly. The system is that a private secretary would mention to the Chief Superintendent in charge that 'so-and-so seems a capable type. Do you think he (or she) might like to cover A, B, or C?' In that way, if the answer is a negative, the Royal is not offended. They do not merely accept the next one on the list. It is not a case of 'Buggins turn' next, but finding someone ideally suited to a particular member of the Royal Family. A police officer who works for the Prince of Wales might be horrified at being moved to Prince Andrew or his brother Edward, and equally, they would dislike the thought of having one of their brother's cast-offs shoved onto them.

CHAPTER NINE

ROYAL BITS AND BOBS

f you really want to upset a member of the Royal Family, any one of them, all you have to do is invite them to open a shop, factory or bazaar and tell them in the letter of invitation that you have already tried someone else and they can't make it.

It is guaranteed to infuriate the Royals as they all see every invitation and decide which ones they are willing to accept.

When Princess Diana was alive she was the number one choice for practically every event, and organisers, in the mistaken belief that there is a central clearing house at Buckingham Palace that allocates engagements around the family, often used to ask if Diana couldn't make it would one of the others stand in for her.

Even today, every member of the Royal Family receives far more invitations than they can accept, and those planning events sometimes still ask the first-choice Royal to pass on the invitation if he or she cannot make it.

The private secretaries of the Prince of Wales, the Duke of York, the Earl of Wessex and the Princess Royal, all have a standard reply that is icily polite but curt, and states, couched in 'Palace speak' that the person inviting their particular Royal should always make it a personal invitation to him or her specifically. In other words, 'We are not in the business of Rent-a-Royal.'

There is a pecking order and in the current Royal Family the Prince of Wales gets the choice of the more glamorous engagements, with the Princess Royal, the hardest working member of the family, receiving those that she has sometimes described as 'less interesting than others'. The second division of the Gloucesters and Kents, including Princess Alexandra, appear to get the leftovers.

The newest Royal couple, the Duke and Duchess of Cambridge, are already being inundated with requests, both for visits and for the Duchess to become President or Patron of hundreds of organisations, both civilian and military. As was proved in their first overseas visit as a married couple, to Canada and the United States, they are being seen as the natural successors to the late Diana, Princess of Wales in the glamour stakes. Back in the United Kingdom, they are effortlessly overtaking the rest of the family as the stars of the future. Instant celebrity is now the name of the game, even among the Royal Family, and the others will inevitably move farther down the league table as William and Catherine gain in confidence and become more accessible. They will soon find out that their relations do not welcome competition – from any source.

On a visit to the United States, a country he adores, the Prince of Wales was addressed by a well-meaning American: 'Hi Prince.' His Royal Highness was not amused and his private secretary was instructed to inform future hosts that if fellow guests could not manage his full title, he would prefer a plain 'Charles'. Anything but 'Hi Prince'.

When Princess Margaret was a child and accompanied her parents on a visit, she often asked her nanny when they returned what the funny smell was wherever they went. The nanny didn't have the heart to tell that the smell was fresh paint and that whenever the King and Queen made a visit, everywhere was painted to make it look like new.

One thing all the members of the Royal Family have learned is how to keep a straight face when meeting people whose knowledge of the background of royalty is perhaps limited. The Princess Royal was on a fund-raising visit to Houston in Texas when one of the major contributors asked her to 'congratulate [her] mother on being re-elected'. She thanked him and promised to pass on his kind remarks.

Diana, Princess of Wales was once asked how her father, Winston Churchill, was keeping. Apart from the obvious error, the person asking the question didn't seem to realise that Churchill had been dead for over thirty years and Diana was then still in her twenties.

Members of the Royal Family, without exception, hate it when guests overstay their welcome, as they themselves are always punctual in arriving, and just as prompt when the time comes for them to leave. Other guests are sometimes reluctant to go, so the family have devised codes to let their servants know when it is time for the guests to leave. They summon a butler and ask if the guest's car has arrived. On hearing this the butler disappears for a moment and then announces that Lord and Lady so-and-so's car is waiting in the drive. The royal host then rises and bids the guests farewell, and it's a very thick-skinned man or woman who doesn't take the hint after that.

A well-trained butler or footman can usually get the better of even the most arrogant visitor. On one occasion, Lord Mountbatten invited his old friend Frank Sinatra to a reception at St James's Palace. When Sinatra arrived he was accompanied by half a dozen of his entourage – all very large, sinister-looking gentlemen. The butler asked to see their invitations, as he knew that Mr Sinatra had been invited to come alone. Sinatra tried to bluff his way in saying, 'They are with me.' The butler stood his ground and refused to allow the bodyguards to enter St James's Palace. Eventually, Sinatra went in on his own and complained to Lord Mountbatten at the high-handed way he had been treated. Mountbatten replied that the butler had been quite right and was only obeying orders. It must have been a rare sight to see the lone figure of the butler standing up to Sinatra's 'heavy mob' – and living to tale the tale. Mountbatten later congratulated the man on his courage.

The domestic staff at Buckingham Palace usually get on quite well with their superiors in the Household. But there have been occasions when they have felt it necessary to make their displeasure known. During a long-haul overseas flight, it is the custom for staff, who have all arrived in their Sunday best, to change into more comfortable, casual clothes for the duration of the flight. They do the changing acts in the privacy of the tiny, cramped lavatories. On one flight to Australia, there was a long queue immediately after take-off, when the Mistress of the Robes, the Duchess of Grafton, pushed her way to the front, claiming senior priority. One self-admitted gay footman, well down the line, exclaimed, in a tone everyone could hear, 'Well, that's the first time I've ever known a Duchess take precedence over a queen.' Her Grace pretended not to hear and continued to the front.

When The Queen and Prince Philip had one of their famous picnics in the grounds of Balmoral, Her Majesty used to like to help with the washing up in the early days. But no longer. At eighty-five who could blame her? But Prince Philip still likes to light the barbecue himself and grill the steaks and sausages – sometimes with unwanted results.

Princess Margaret also liked to think she was domesticated when she was courting Antony Armstrong Jones. Visiting him at his studio in London's Docklands, she would try a little dusting and cleaning and washing the occasional plate, but once they were married, that all ended. She didn't want to do it and neither did her staff at Kensington Palace want any interference. She also didn't care for gardening, unlike her husband who enjoyed getting his hands dirty – and The Queen Mother, who said you couldn't call yourself a real gardener if you didn't get some earth under your fingernails.

When The Queen was crowned in Westminster Abbey on 2 June 1953, a total of 8,251 guests were accommodated in the church, the largest number ever, with every one seated.

Among the older generation of Royals, the late Princess Marina, mother of the present Duke of Kent, had an annual ritual where she would insist on cleaning her collection of bone china. But even here everything was laid on for her, as her former butler, Peter Russell, explained in his book, *Butler Royal*:

> A maid and butler would prepare several bowls of warm, soapy water with clean tea towels at hand. Then fresh kitchen gloves, liberally sprinkled with talcum powder inside to make them easy to put on, were handed to the Princess. Once she was ready, she would wash every item and hand it to her maid to dry.

The entire operation lasted a couple of hours and Marina couldn't afterwards understand why all the housework couldn't be as meticulous, not realising, of course, that if the staff took as long as she did – just once a year – they would never finish their everyday chores.

Apart from this little example of domesticity, Marina never ventured behind the green baize door and she was said to be an insufferable snob, which was unkind as her values were those of someone who had grown up surrounded by royalty and to whom it would never have occurred to mix socially with 'ordinary' men and women. When she heard that Princess Margaret was to marry Antony Armstrong Jones, she remarked, 'How strange for the daughter of an Emperor to be marrying a subject.' It wasn't even an original opinion. The comment was first attributed to Queen Mary when her daughter Mary, the Princess Royal, married Henry, Viscount Lascelles (later 6th Earl of Harewood).

And during the early days of the Second World War, when Britain was suffering the blitz bombing raids night after night, Marina's private secretary still found time to correspond with the manager of a munitions factory the Princess was due to visit, stressing that it was important for women to remove their protective gloves when being presented.

It is a common assumption that every member of the Royal Family is rich. And while it is true that they all live in surroundings that would be considered beyond many people's wildest dreams, this is mainly through the generosity of The Queen. She provides Grace and Favour homes to all her relations, even if, in recent years she has been forced to increase rents to a level where, for instance, Prince and Princess Michael of Kent, are now required to pay £120,000 a year for their magnificent apartment in Kensington Palace.

But while The Queen's children have all been the recipients of large trust funds, so they will never have to worry about finding the rent or paying Household bills, it hasn't always been the case that being Royal meant unlimited wealth.

When Princess Marina, Duchess of Kent, died in 1968, her will revealed that she left an estate of £76,186 gross, which was reduced by liabilities to £54,121 net. Out of this figure, which was fairly respectable for the time, massive death duties at 67 per cent brought the final figure down to £17,398, the smallest amount ever left by a member of the Royal Family.

This was the sum that was divided between her three children, Eddie (the present Duke of Kent), Princess Alexandra and Prince Michael.

The main reason for the huge percentage of death duties (now called Inheritance Tax) was that Marina had made certain settlements on former employees whom she felt obliged to support, but the gifts had been made within the seven-year exclusion period which meant they were all liable for tax. The same seven-year rule applies today; any gift made over seven years before the donor dies is exempt from tax; any gift made within six years and three hundred and sixty-four days is taxed at 40 per cent.

So Princess Marina, who didn't have a fortune to begin with, ended her life practically a pauper, just through her own generosity, and the ones to suffer were her own children. However, she need not have remained one of the poor relations. In 1957 she could have become a queen when Crown Prince Olaf of Norway proposed to her, using The Queen Mother as an intermediary. This was the same year that Olaf became King of Norway. Marina thanked him for his offer but gently turned him down saying she was devoting the rest of her life to the welfare of her children.

The Prince of Wales is particular about everything. He enjoys cheese and biscuits to end a meal, with both coming from his Duchy of Cornwall estate. He likes his biscuits to be served at a special temperature and the staff keep a warming pan just to maintain them at the perfect level.

If any of his silver or jewellery needs repairs or servicing, the article is despatched to Cartier or Garrard, the Crown Jewellers. They are always accompanied by an armed police officer and it is always one of the male staff that carries them. No female servant is permitted to handle the precious articles in case she is attacked.

The Crown Jewellers keep detailed photographs of every important piece of silver and jewellery, so that if one piece becomes badly damaged, they will know what they should look like when restored.

The Queen keeps 100 dozen bottles of Krug champagne in her cellars – even though she loathes the stuff herself – and countless more cases of every other vintage brand. There is a bottle of cognac said to be worth £10,000, as it's the only one of its kind left in the world. There were four: one was opened by Queen Victoria to celebrate her Silver Jubilee; another by King Edward VII on his sixty-fifth birthday, while the third was drunk by King George VI and Winston Churchill (who was said to have consumed more than half of it himself) at the end of the Second World War in 1945. The Palace is expecting the next royal milestone to be toasted with this exquisite and unique liqueur to fall in February 2012 – the celebration of Her Majesty's Diamond Jubilee.

CHAPTER TEN

PAY CHEQUES

ewcomers to the Palace – footmen and housemaids – start on a basic salary of £13,634 a year, which can rise after five years by £2,000 a year. On promotion to Senior Footman, a salary of £15,634 is paid which is the same as the three Head Housemaids. At the time of writing, the Palace is advertising for a Butler with an annual salary of £15,000 plus accommodation, and for a Liveried Helper in the Royal Mews, who is required to have had some experience with horses and who will be seen riding behind The Queen on one of the State Carriages at official ceremonial occasions. The starting salary for this post is £17,169, with the livery provided. They are also looking for people to take on casual work in the ticket offices at £7.75 an hour.

In the Royal kitchens, qualified staff earn more than their colleagues on the other side of the green baize door. A sous chef could be paid up to £18,256 while senior chefs rise to £27,218.

The Queen's Royal Chef is the highest paid member of the domestic Household with an annual salary of £45,000.

His opposite number in the liveried staff is the Palace Steward, the senior member of the Master of the Household's domestic staff. Having worked his way up from being a junior footman over twenty years ago, the Palace Steward now earns around £30,000 a year while his deputy, the Page of the Chambers, is paid only slightly less.

In other departments, for example the Royal Collection, there is a different grading system, with almost every employee being a graduate. The Administrator of the Collection earns around £30,000, while, at the time of writing, they need an official in the Human Resources branch with a starting salary between £30,000 and £35,000.

The most profitable section of the Royal Collection is the Enterprises department that arranges exhibitions and retail sales and the person responsible whose title is Managing Director Royal Enterprises earns over £70,000 a year plus a performance related bonus.

The Queen's press secretary is not among the highest paid members of her Household, being paid a salary of £65,000 a year, with her staff of thirteen on considerably less. The information officers who handle many of the day-to-day enquiries, all earn around £30,000.

A bone of contention among Palace staff is the amount they are paid in relation to the salaries of their opposite numbers in Clarence House, working for the Prince of Wales.

The Prince's private secretary is the highest paid member of the entire Household, earning more than twice that paid to The Queen's private secretary. But his salary of £300,000 is still not considered over generous by men and women with similar responsibilities in the City; most of whom wouldn't get out of bed for that sort of money.

Prince Charles's press secretary, who once worked for Sir Alex Ferguson at Manchester United, is paid three times the salary of The Queen's press secretary, and in view of the times he has to justify his boss's expenditure to the public and media, some would say he is worth every penny.

In the early years of her reign, The Queen provided accommodation for everyone who worked for her, free of charge. That has all changed and today 17.5 per cent of everyone's salary is deducted to pay for living accommodation.

When you look at the rent the Prince of Wales's private secretary pays for his house within Kensington Palace – £52,500 a year, or a little over a £1,000 a week – it seems excessive at first, even for a man on £6,000 a week. But he still pays four times more than either the Duke of York pays for Royal Lodge, or the Earl of Wessex for Bagshot Park.

The people who are hardest hit though are those at the lower end of the salary scale. If that Liveried Helper in the Royal Mews is allocated a flat, he will have the usual 17.5 per cent of his salary deducted. Which means in real terms he will pay around £2,900 a year or just under £60 a week, out of his weekly wage of a little over £320 – a sizable sum.

In addition to the rent they pay, those tenants of The Queen who occupy self-contained accommodation, including members of the Royal Family, pay their own council tax. There is one exception: the Royal chaplains, who are not liable for council tax under special arrangements made for the clergy.

Of course, one has to remember that the properties occupied by staff and members of the Royal Household, are in some of the most sought after areas in Britain. Not only those in London, but at Windsor where a large number of staff have been given the use of mews cottages, flats and houses, with one or two, including Adelaide Cottage (which is nothing like the image one usually has of a chocolate-box cottage; more an elegant country home) is presently the residence of the former Director of the Royal Collection (he still lives there as his wife is the Royal Librarian at Windsor Castle and the tenancy has been transferred to her name). Situated in Windsor Home Park, Adelaide Cottage must be worth several million if placed on the open market.

The Grace and Favour home in Kensington Palace, currently the London home of the Duke and Duchess of Cambridge (who are not obliged to pay rent) was previously occupied by the private secretary to the Duke of Edinburgh, and he was required to pay both rent and council tax.

The Queen is a loyal landlord, and a number of her former staff, or their widows, live rent-free in apartments in elegant surroundings such as Hampton Court Palace, where there is an absolute warren of flats, houses and apartments. The majority of these tenants are elderly and some complain (but never to Her Majesty) about the draughty conditions in these ancient buildings.

One of the most gracious Grace and Favour properties in Hampton Court Palace is Wilderness House, just opposite the Maze. The late Lord [Chips] Maclean, the former Lord Chamberlain, was granted the tenancy of the house when he retired from full-time Household duties and was appointed Constable of Hampton Court Palace, a sinecure that made few demands on his time.

Lord Maclean died in 1990 and since then his widow has remained the sole occupant of this magnificent property, which is complete with its own ballroom.

The Household employs a number of temporary staff: footmen, waiters and kitchen operatives, when a banquet or reception is planned at the Palace. They need to have had a certain amount of experience and the Deputy Master of the Household, who controls these affairs, knows who will be available and where to contact them.

The money is basic, around £5.50 an hour, with a meal thrown in for good measure. But the jobs are casual and the men and women who take them on are usually employed in catering elsewhere and can manage to get the time off. Hotel and restaurant managers quite like the idea of their staff serving royalty at Buckingham Palace or Windsor Castle.

A full-time assistant in the Windsor Farm Shop is employed on an hourly basis, thirty-nine hours a week at £6.40 an hour.

Within the domestic Household there are several grades of servant: footmen, senior footmen, sergeant footmen, Page of the Presence and Page of the Chambers, valets, Yeomen, Travelling Yeomen, house-maids, senior housemaids and dressers.

Every one of these is at the lower end of the pay scale. Even the Chief Housekeeper, who supervises the thirteen housemaids, is paid less than £30,000, while Her Majesty's dressers, her closest personal servants are paid on the same scale as the senior housemaids.

In between the housemaids and seniors are the Housekeeping Supervisors. These ladies oversee up to four Housekeeping Assistants each. One looks after the 'Chamber' or second floor of the Palace where the staff bedrooms are located. The Supervisors earn £15,000 with the assistants on a starting salary of £13,000.

In the Royal Mews, where there is a healthy rivalry between the garage staff, who look after the vehicles, and those whose work consists of grooming the horses and maintaining the carriages.

The mechanics and chauffeurs are all qualified men (The Queen does not employ any female chauffeurs) and this is reflected in their pay scale.

The head chauffeur is paid over £28,000 a year with the mechanics and engineers earning only slightly less.

In the stables, as we have seen, a Liveried Helper, the most junior member of the team, starts on a little over £17,000 a year, with yearly increases.

The senior carriage drivers; they are the men who control the horses pulling the State carriages on formal occasions, are paid between £20,000 and £25,000 a year.

The attendants who are seen riding on the rear of the carriages can be Liveried Helpers or Footmen who have been trained for this duty. But only one of the men is a member of the Royal Household, the man always seen immediately behind The Queen is a police bodyguard, wearing an identical livery to the attendant for obvious reasons – but not on the same money.

The gardens at Buckingham Palace are immaculate, as one would expect. Covering thirty-nine acres, with a 150-metre herbaceous border and a lake where black swans once swam before they were all killed by marauding urban foxes, eleven gardeners work full-time maintaining the flowerbeds and massive lawns in pristine condition.

The Palace has a system for training gardeners, employing a number of youngsters as apprentices. They are paid between £12,000 and £14,000 a year, with an increase to £16,000 when they qualify to work unsupervised.

Clerical staff and office managers are paid according to their rank and responsibilities.

Accountants in the Privy Purse Office, the Personnel and Pensions managers and the Master of the Household's senior office staff earn between £30,000 and £56,000.

The salary scale for typists, secretaries and clerks, is between £18,000 and £25,000.

Everyone is taxed at source; nobody is employed on contract and there are no self-employed men or women in the Royal Household.

All expenses are scrutinised, as transparency is the policy in all Palace finances. Senior staff travel first class by rail in Britain and business class when flying abroad on Royal duties.

In terms of sheer value for money, the Royal Household is among the most efficient business organisations in the country, if not in the world. If staff were on overtime or piecework rates the wage bills would be astronomical. But dedicated servants, both domestic and clerical, work literally hundreds of extra hours because they regard themselves as professionals with a remarkable capacity for hard work.

The Queen is aware that the majority of her Household could more than double their salary if they decided to work elsewhere, in industry or commerce, and she appreciates their loyalty.

What she doesn't offer is more money. Her Majesty is restricted by the amount she receives from the Civil List and while her senior aides, those in charge of the six main departments, could hardly be said to be on the bread line, those right at the bottom of the pay chain, still languish on wages and salaries that are below the national average.

Even so, a footman who just ten years ago would have been lucky to get £100 a week, is now paid nearly £300 a week – and together with all the other benefits – laundry, heating, light, meals and subsided drinks – there is no shortage of young men and women who are willing to spend a few years in the service of the Monarch – mainly in the hope of moving to a better paid job later.

Some of the traditionalists in the Royal Household cannot accept that accountants, to whom the cardinal sin is for a department to go into the red, now run the Palace.

The days when money didn't matter are long gone and are over for good. Just as in any other business, the bottom line must be profitability and The Queen's Keeper of the Privy Purse is without doubt the most cost-conscious person in Buckingham Palace. Some of his practices may be unpopular but, in the long run, his word is law and as far as he is concerned the ends always justify the means.

CHAPTER ELEVEN

THE QUEEN'S AND PRINCE CHARLES'S MONEY

No one doubts that The Queen is a wealthy woman, with a fortune that has been allowed to accumulate through decades of sound advice and monetary shrewdness by her financial advisers in banking and the City.

She has also benefited from tax privileges available only to her and not to any of her people. In spite of all these advantages, The Queen is not the richest person in the United Kingdom, or even the richest woman. Estimates of her wealth vary from £100 million to over £1 billion, but those people who, in spite of arguments to the contrary, still believe that she owns all her palaces and castles, and every piece of the Crown Jewels, none of which is her personal property, really have no idea.

There is a vast difference between the sovereign's private wealth and the riches of the Crown, which are inalienable and have to be passed down from generation to generation. The only properties The Queen could sell in her own right are Balmoral Castle and Sandringham House. But before one imagines that might put her on the bread line, it should be remembered that those two properties have a combined value in excess of £100 million.

The private incomes of The Queen and the Prince of Wales are paid by the Duchy of Lancaster and the Duchy of Cornwall, the two exceptions when George III surrendered the monarch's land to the Crown Estate in 1760 in return for a Civil List.

Both these estates are fabulously wealthy and as the recipients of the proceeds, The Queen's and her eldest son's fortunes increase year by year as they are managed by some of the sharpest financial brains in the world.

No accurate estimate of either Elizabeth II's or the Prince of Wales's true worth has ever been revealed – and neither will it ever be. But, assisted by the transparency of the financial accounts that are published every year, it is possible to arrive at a reasonably educated valuation.

THE DUCHY OF LANCASTER

The estate of the Duchy of Lancaster consists of large areas of land in Lancashire (where The Queen is known as the 'Duke' of Lancaster not Duchess),

Yorkshire, Lincolnshire, Northamptonshire, Cheshire, Shropshire and Staffordshire, plus the most valuable single freehold of all – the ground on which stands the Savoy Hotel in The Strand in London's West End.

In 2010 the assets of the Duchy amounted to £350 million, up from a little over £200 million ten years ago. And in the same year (2010) The Queen received some £13.2 million in income from the profits of the Duchy.

The Duchy itself does not pay tax but income from the Privy Purse to Her Majesty is taxed at normal rates after expenses have been deducted.

Even so, if the Sovereign had retained the entire Crown Estates and relinquished the two Duchies: Lancaster and Cornwall, they would both have been far better off as the income for the Crown Estates in 2009/2010 amounted to a staggering £298 million.

Council appointed by her manages the estates of the Duchy of Lancaster on behalf of Her Majesty and the Government of the day also keeps a close eye on its affairs through the office of Chancellor of the Duchy of Lancaster. This office is usually held by a minister of the Crown appointed by the Prime Minister and so changes with each Government. The main responsibility of the Chancellor is approving the annual accounts.

Apart from the monetary advantages to The Queen as Duke of Lancaster, she also enjoys certain other rights such as appointing High Sheriffs in Lancashire, Greater Manchester and Merseyside. These are separate appointments to those made for the rest of England and Wales, and The Queen uses a bodkin to 'prick' the names offered to her by the Chancellor. The tradition of using a bodkin goes back to the reign of Elizabeth I, who when she was due to pick a High Sheriff, found she didn't have a pen handy, so used her own bodkin instead. It is from such inconsequential trivialities that ancient customs are derived.

Another of The Queen's patronages is the right to bestow livings to clergy in forty-two parishes within her Duchy, though strangely, none at all in Lancaster itself. These church livings range from Yorkshire to Avon, Essex to Lincolnshire, Norfolk to Gloucestershire and Leicestershire to Durham.

For over 600 years the Duke of Lancaster also had the right to appoint magistrates, but this long tradition came to an end in 2005 under the Courts Act 2003, and now it is the responsibility of the Ministry of Justice.

One tradition that has remained is *Bona Vacantia* or the right of the Duchy of Lancaster to the estate of anyone who dies having not left a will.

However, if anyone can prove that they have a reasonable claim to all or part of an estate, the Solicitor for the Duchy is authorised to pass it on as a 'gift' from the Duke of Lancaster.

Anything remaining – and all the other unclaimed legacies – is channelled into two charities: The Duchy of Lancaster Benevolent Fund and The Duchy of Lancaster Jubilee Trust.

When one reads in the annual accounts of Royal Finances that The Queen has returned to the Treasury amounts paid to members of her family, the money will have come from her income from the Duchy of Lancaster.

She also uses part of the income to pay for the upkeep of her private homes: Sandringham and Balmoral, which are hers and are not paid for by the taxpayer.

All other personal expenses, such as her clothes (apart from those worn on official engagements, both at home and on overseas tours, which are the responsibility of various Government departments) and her racing expenses, are met from this single source of income.

CHAPTER TWELVE

THE DUCHY OF CORNWALL

Prince Charles owns next to nothing in his own name. His houses, cars even his suits, shoes and shirts are all provided by the Duchy of Cornwall, the estate created for Edward the Black Prince in 1337, and which since that date has provided an income for every Prince of Wales. For those interested in such facts, there have been twenty-three other Princes of Wales who have held the title Duke of Cornwall.

So, when Charles bought Highgrove House in 1980 as a country home, together with 347 acres of farmland, the cheque for around £800,000 was signed by an official of the Duchy of Cornwall, and His Royal Highness's name does not appear anywhere on the deeds of the property. Similarly, if it were to be sold, with all the extra land he has bought in addition – even though it would be on the instructions of

Charles – the Duchy would profit from the deal and not him personally.

If there is no son or grandson to inherit the Duchy, a daughter is not eligible. So when The Queen was Princess Elizabeth and had no brothers, her father, King George VI, received the income from the Duchy, which he then used to provide incomes for his brothers, the Dukes of Gloucester and Kent.

Prince Charles has received the benefit of the profits of the Duchy of Cornwall since he came of age. The state comprises nearly 130,000 acres and is spread mainly over twenty counties in England but surprisingly, only one in his Principality of Wales.

Outside London, the largest single parcel of land owned by the Duchy is 70,000 acres of Dartmoor, on which the notorious Prison stands. So Charles is, in effect, Dartmoor's landlord.

But the forty-odd acres the Duchy owns in London is easily the most valuable in the entire portfolio. Houses, blocks of flats and offices in Kennington are worth millions, with the Oval cricket ground, home to Surrey County Cricket Club, the single jewel in this particular crown. Charles, as landlord, is given a private Royal box in the ground, adorned with the Prince of Wales's feathers, but as he has little interest in cricket, he has rarely made use of this unique privilege.

The remainder of the estate includes the following holdings:

Cornwall	72,489 acres
Devon	21,546 acres
Isle of Scilly	3,984 acres

Avon	8,919 acres
Somerset	7,735 acres
Wiltshire	3,769 acres
Dorset	2,798 acres
Lincolnshire	1,936 acres
Gloucestershire	1,864 acres
South Glamorgan	700 acres

All of which makes Prince Charles, through the Duchy of Cornwall, a very rich man indeed. But its capital is inalienable, so he cannot sell any part of it for his personal gain. It must be passed on to the next Prince of Wales.

The Duchy's property interests range far and wide and includes pubs, office blocks, farms and small businesses. Two hundred and forty tenants rent farms (with the smallest being a ten-acre holding on the Isles of Scilly, with the largest, a 1,600-acre farm on Dartmoor) while there are 1,500 in residential accommodation. The portfolio includes 160 miles of foreshore with mineral rights to a further 230,000 acres.

There are one or two strange privileges attached to being Duke of Cornwall, the inhabitants of the Isles of Scilly are required to provide him with 300 puffins every year. No one knows if he has exercised this right as yet. He also has the right to the carcass of any whale that is washed up on his foreshore – and he is legally obliged to dispose of said bodies.

The property and assets of anyone who dies in the Duchy without making a will are passed to the Duchy of Cornwall and it is surprising how much money is raised in this way. All the proceeds are disposed of through a number of the Prince's charities.

In order to receive the benefits of the Duchy, the Duke of Cornwall has to undergo an archaic and somewhat embarrassing ritual before being accepted by the people of the county.

In 1973, Prince Charles duly arrived at the ruins of Launceston Castle (one of six the Duchy owns in Cornwall) to take part in a centuries-old ceremony to secure his seigneurial rights.

In keeping with ancient custom, he was presented with: a load of firewood, a grey clock, 100 shillings (a shilling is five pence in today's currency), a pound of pepper, a hunting bow, a pair of gilt spurs, a pound of herbs, a salmon spear, a pair of falconer's gauntlets and two greyhounds.

After symbolically accepting the gifts – without having the least idea what they were all to be used for – the Duke of Cornwall directed that they be returned to Launceston Museum where they are on view to the public. The greyhounds, which were on loan, went back to their rightful owner.

A Council with Prince Charles as Chairman administers the Duchy of Cornwall. But he is not just a rubber-stamp figure and he refuses to accept that the prime responsibility of the Duchy is to maximise its profits.

On a number of occasions, the professionals who advise him on the Council have been over-ruled when they have pointed out that it is uneconomical to continue with some of the tiny tenanted farms and smallholdings. He refuses to raise rents or to combine several smaller properties into larger holdings simply because it makes more business sense. Displaying a deep feeling of social responsibility, he manages a delicate balancing act between commercial profitability and concern for his tenants' welfare, knowing that if he allowed any unpopular moves against his tenants, the media would crucify him.

One thing Prince William can be sure of is that when the time comes for his father to hand over the reins – and profits – of the Duchy of Cornwall to him, they will be in excellent condition.

EPILOGUE

Epilogue

obody in his or her right mind, even the most dyed-in-the-wool Royalist, would ever dare claim that the Monarchy is run on the cheap.

As the Sovereign is seen as being apart from her people, and should be seen to be so, it follows that Her Majesty, and the institution she represents, should be maintained in a manner that is regal and therefore necessarily expensive.

Few would argue that The Queen is profligate. She does not indulge in frivolous or extravagant past-times (those who say her racing interests are merely a rich woman's pleasures paid for by the taxpayers, find it difficult to accept that she pays every penny out of her own pocket and nothing comes out of the public purse) and her personal tastes reflect those of an upper-class country woman rather than a spoilt monarch who can have anything she wants merely by lifting a Royal digit.

The British Monarchy is cost-effective. In the United States, the cost of maintaining the President and the White House is far greater than the combined cost of the Monarchy and the Prime Minister in Britain.

Of course, one could argue that the White House is the seat of Government, and the Administration of such an enormous country, with the richest economy in the world, requires a larger budget. It is interesting to note that the Press Office at the White House employs more people than the entire Royal Household, and the security detail for this single property and one married couple and their children, far outnumbers the Royalty and Diplomatic Department of the Metropolitan Police, which guards every diplomatic mission in London as well as the Royal Family.

Nevertheless it has long been a bone of contention that The Queen and her family cost the British taxpayers far too much money. And it is true that the entire cost is borne by Britain; the Commonwealth countries, even those of which The Queen is head of state, do not contribute a penny towards the upkeep of the monarchy.

Many republicans believe that the Monarchy underpins a class-conscious nation that refuses to move into the twenty-first century and prefers the idea of living in the past. They also say the Monarchy is interested only in its own survival, not the interests of the United Kingdom or its population. It's an argument that has little support from the majority of British people.

Public interest in the Royal Family continues unabated. The wedding of Prince William and Catherine Middleton proved that where 'ordinary' men and women are concerned there is a huge groundswell of affection and goodwill towards royalty. Otherwise why would hundreds of thousands of people camp out all night in London just to catch a glimpse of the couple on their way to and from Westminster Abbey? And their first overseas tour, to Canada and the United States, proved that there is still a fascination with all things Royal, with a media frenzy matched only by tens of thousands of fans – and that is the only word that can truly describe the onlookers who turned out to greet William and Catherine – everywhere they went. Hollywood's own 'royalty' took second place to the real thing.

William and Catherine have already, in the short space of a few months, established their credentials as block-busting celebrities. So, if public popularity is the yardstick by which the success or otherwise of the Monarchy is measured, the race is already won.

Would this have happened if it had been just a film star or sports celebrity? Hardly. There is something very special about the British Royal Family that sets them apart from everyone else, even other monarchies. The late President Ronald Reagan summed it up perfectly when he said, 'With respect to every other king or queen in the world, when we speak about "The Queen" we all know which one we are talking about.' He meant, of course, Elizabeth II.

The Queen has been on the throne for sixty years and throughout that time every national poll has indicated that the Monarchy remains the single most popular institution in Britain.

There have been occasional blips, particularly in 1997 over the death of the late Diana, Princess of Wales, when the Royal Family in general and The Queen in particular, were accused of treating her with too little sympathy and understanding and thereby indirectly being the cause of the tragedy.

The wave of anti-Royal feeling lasted only for a few days, but at the time it caused deep concern among the family. There remains some feeling of antipathy towards the Duke and Duchess of Cornwall in a few parts of the world. But as the years pass, attitudes soften and Charles and Camilla have become accepted as a happily married couple. Eventually even the romantic image of Diana will gradually fade from public memory, as today, most of the younger generation cannot understand what all the fuss was about when Charles and Diana divorced.

Since 1952 when Elizabeth II ascended the Throne, Britain's reputation as an industrial and manufacturing nation has steadily declined, yet the influence of the Monarchy, through the person of The Queen, has grown immeasurably.

Where our political power has diminished, Her Majesty's influence has increased, to the position where it is now one of the few aspects of Britain that still commands international admiration and respect.

Part of that success must be that The Queen, the most experienced head of state in the world, treats everyone the same. She is a great leveller, with no favourites. Prime Ministers and Presidents,

Archbishops and Artisans; all receive exactly the same courteous greeting – and all are kept at arms length! She makes no distinction between her subjects and the heads of state of any other country, no matter how powerful or otherwise they may be.

There is a mistaken belief that because The Queen comes from such a rarefied background, she is only comfortable among others from similar, if not the same, origins: affluent aristocrats from ancient families. This is totally untrue. The Royal Family lives in a social category entirely its own. But as a pragmatist, The Queen realises that no longer is it possible to expect social intercourse and even inter-marriage between European royalty exclusively as it once was.

Hence the acceptance of The Queen's granddaughter marrying, with her blessing, a lower middle-class lad from Yorkshire, who happens to play rugby for his country, and doesn't speak with a cut-glass accent.

Britain's Royal Family is unique in that its senior members 'The Firm', who undertake public duties, are not expected to involve themselves in any outside commercial activities (with the possible exception of the Prince of Wales and his Duchy of Cornwall enterprises).

While their European counterparts in Norway, Denmark, Sweden, Belgium and The Netherlands all work (and travel on public transport) it would be unthinkable for the Duke of Edinburgh (in his early days) or the Princess Royal to be associated with outside businesses while still receiving money from public funds.

The junior and 'semi-detached' members like Prince Michael of Kent, Sir Tim Laurence, Peter and Zara Phillips are required to earn a living, but as they are not involved in Royal affairs, no one objects. In fact, if they didn't engage in productive employment, critics would soon lump them together as 'free-loading' Royals.

The Royal Household is far from perfect, with too many servants fervently holding the belief that royalty is infallible in all things. When in reality they are just as liable as the rest of us to commit sins and errors – it's just that they will never admit to their mistakes, they simply ignore them.

There is a seamless continuity about the Household that ensures its stability. In the many years I have been a visitor to Buckingham Palace on a frequent though irregular basis, I have seen a number of changes – not all of them improvements.

One thing that has struck me quite forcibly is the lack of individual personalities one meets in the Palace corridors these days. There's a sameness about the people who work there. There used to be the odd eccentric who was tolerated because The Queen and the Duke of Edinburgh liked having them around, so their little peccadilloes were accepted. All that seems to have disappeared. Efficiency has replaced enthusiasm, which I suppose makes for a smoother running operation. But in an organisation as large as the Royal Household surely there could still be a place for the occasional oddball?

The Queen and Prince Philip are in the autumn of their lives. Her Majesty is twenty-five years past the official retiring age for women, while her husband could have claimed his old age pension (if he was entitled to one) some thirty years ago. Both have senior rail cards with Prince Philip having his blown up to poster size that now adorns one of the walls in his saloon on the Royal Train.

They have both fulfilled their roles with flawless professionalism for sixty years and they have proved, that in the institution of Monarchy, Britain and the Commonwealth has certainly got value for money.

There is no one working at Buckingham Palace who was there when Elizabeth II came to the throne as a twenty-five-year-old Queen in 1952. Her current Prime Minister, David Cameron, wasn't even born when she was crowned. She is the constant presence who has ensured the stability of the Monarchy through some turbulent periods: the Falklands Campaign, Britain's involvement in Iraq and Afghanistan, domestic recession, devolution and the divorces of three of her children.

So if Her Majesty seeks comfort from time to time in the company of her Corgis, who can blame her? Even if they are yappy, snappy, hated by most of the Household and apt to nip at the ankles of unwary footmen.

SELECT BIBLIOGRAPHY

Among the books consulted are:

Royal Encyclopedia, ed. Ronald Allison & Sarah Riddell, Macmillan, 1991

Inside Buckingham Palace, Andrew Morton, Michael O'Mara Books, 1991

At Home With The Queen, Brian Hoey, HarperCollins, 2003

The New Royal Court, Brian Hoey, Sidgewick & Jackson, 1990

Royal Service, Stephen Barry, Macmillan, 1983

Butler Royal, Peter Russell, Hutchinson, 1983

The Final Curtsey, Margaret Rhodes, Calder Walker Associates, 2011

My Mountbatten Years, William Evans, Headline, 1989

HRH Princess Anne, Brian Hoey, Country Life Books, 1984